Love, Harry Jr.

Patch of the 76th Division

Love, Harry Jr.

– A World War II Soldier Writes Home –

Hamilton Harry B.

Compiled by MARTHA KAY COLE

The Wooster Book Company
Wooster Ohio • 2001

The Wooster Book Company
where minds and imaginations meet
205 West Liberty Street
Wooster Ohio • 44691

© 2001 Martha Kay Cole
  All rights reserved.
  Printed in the Untied States of America.

ISBN: 1-888683-44-9

Cover design by Wendy Cole.

My father, Harry B. Hamilton, Jr.

—*Martha Kay Cole*

Contents

Introduction

Love, Harry Jr. is a collection of letters I wrote to my mother and father, Martha and Harry B. Hamilton, Sr. I was their only child and enlisted in the U.S. Army in April 1944. I was 24 years old, married and had a 3-year-old daughter. After being inducted into the army on May 11, 1944, at Fort Benjamin Harrison in Indianapolis, Indiana, I was sent by train to Camp Croft, South Carolina, on May 13, 1944, for 13 weeks of basic training. That is where the letters begin.

After a ten-day furlough at home and about six more weeks of training at Camp McCoy, Wisconsin, I was sent to Camp Miles Standish near Boston, Massachusetts, and shipped out on Thanksgiving Day, November 23, 1944. We arrived at Plymouth, England, December 4, to become a part of the 76th Division of General Patton's Third Army.

As an account of a Private First Class, I saw action in France, Belgium, Luxembourg and Germany, including the Battle of the Bulge.

Many thanks to my beloved wife Kay and my daughter Martha Kay Cole for their guidance and assurance that these letters should be made known.

An Appreciation

Love, Harry Jr. began on Christmas day, 1998. Like many families, we celebrate Christmas at Grandma and Grandpa's house. But that year it wasn't quite the same. Grandpa was temporarily hospitalized and was unable to join us. Our visit with him in the hospital only seemed to make Christmas dinner back at the house a little less gloomy, even in spite of the array of family-favorite dishes and desserts Grandma had prepared. Perhaps sensing our mood, or perhaps thinking of another Christmas when Grandpa was absent, Grandma climbed the stairs to the attic and returned with a box full of letters he had written to his parents during World War II.

Grandpa's place at the table wasn't the only absence the letters began to fill. We all knew that Grandpa had fought in the Battle of the Bulge, which also started around Christmas of 1944 and remains the bloodiest battle in U.S. military history. Over the years, though, he never said much about his experiences, except for off-the-cuff observations like, "You'd be surprised what you'd eat if you were hungry enough." And whenever we asked him about the war, he usually would only say, "We were surrounded for awhile; but we escaped." But after we had read the letters, he became more willing to answer questions and tell more detailed stories (many of which appear in the Epilogue). I'll never forget his vivid description of crossing an icy river into Germany to attack the Siegfried Line. An eighteen-year-old soldier next to him let go of the raft and let himself sink, choosing suicide rather than facing the Germans waiting on the other side. "He couldn't have been more scared than I was," Grandpa said at story's end with a finality that gave us the feeling that enough had been said.

I think what impressed me about the way Grandpa told that story was the same thing that impressed me about Harry Jr. and his letters. The first few introduce a young man eagerly beginning boot camp and anticipating the greatest adventure of his life. As the fighting in Europe looms closer, however, reality sets in with thoughts of his parents and his wife and three-year-old daughter. Harry Jr. could be pretty resourceful in reassuring the folks at home. Since censorship prevented him from revealing his exact whereabouts, he wrote acrostic sentences like "Buy our stock to offset November sales," to signal to his parents (who never bought or sold stock) that he was in Boston preparing to cross over to England. A few letters later, he signals in a similar manner that he has arrived in Bournemouth, his last stop before going to the front. Clever as such moments are, what's truly striking throughout the letters is Harry Jr.'s firm determination to face and overcome whatever the war threw at him and finally to return home to his family.

Another fascinating feature of many of the letters are the repeated thank-yous for letters and items received and ardent requests to keep the letters coming. Clearly, the ongoing exchange of letters was a crucial lifeline for Grandpa. In the current age of telephones and e-mail, it's amazing to realize that, besides the letters that make up this volume, he also wrote scores of letters to Grandma and corresponded with several other relatives and friends.

Some of that industriousness was apparently passed down to my mother, Martha Kay Hamilton Cole, who worked tirelessly and ceaselessly for nearly three years to bring this project to completion. Once again, and for different reasons, I'm starting to sense that enough has been said. With their unique glimpse into the experience of a World War II foot soldier, the letters can certainly speak for themselves.

—Dan Cole

INDIANAPOLIS, IND.
MAY 6
5-PM
1944

H. B. Hamilton
205 W. Liberty St.
Ashland, O.

Hi Pop & Mom!
Arrived at 7:15 your time - 6:15 here, my address is

Pvt. Harry B. Hamilton Jr.
Co. D. Barracks 4
Reception Center
Fort Ben. Harrison
Indianapolis Ind.

Everything O.K. Lights out at 9:00 have to be off street at 11:00! Have not been sworn in yet.

D mshal is sleeping beside me. This address is temporary. Write if you can. I'll be here 5 or 10 days.
Love Harry

Basic Training

Wednesday Night 8:30 P.M.
May 17, 1944

Hi Mom & Dad:

How are you all by now? I am fine and dandy. It is hot down here. It hasn't been under 90 yet. I am getting brown and I weigh 142 lbs. stripped. So I have gained 4 1/2 or 5 lbs. since I left home. My legs and arms are a little sore tonight. We had setting up exercises this morning for the first time and it has got all of our muscles in knots. They really feed us good here. We can always go back and get more after we finish the first plateful.

I just got done taking a shower, washing my head, shaving and brushing my teeth. I also washed 2 pair of shorts, 3 handkerchiefs, 1 pair of sox and 1 fatigue pants and 1 fatigue shirt. I am going to bed pretty soon and get a good night's sleep.

Will you please tell Kay to send me a couple of bars of Lifebuoy soap? I can't buy any here & I want some. I suppose you know that I started smoking again. Not much though, just 4 or 5 cigarettes a day. I can buy Camels or any other kind for 12 cents a pack. It helps a fellow out a lot while you are setting around.

I wrote a letter to Kay this noon and another one at 5:30. I haven't had much of a chance to write to anyone else but I'll get around to them all pretty soon.

This place is really nice. It is a whole lot better than Ft. Benjamin On the way down we saw roses in full bloom and thousands of wild flowers. We went by hundreds of peach orchards and it won't be long until the peaches will be starting.

We were issued a steel helmet and a gas mask today. Yesterday we rolled field packs and pitched pup tents. We spend about 4 or 5 hours a day out in the drill field and they sure do put us through the paces. We had a parade at 4:30 today and we marched by and were reviewed by 2 majors and our platoon was the best in the whole outfit. The majors came around and told us so afterwards. It really makes a fellow feel good when he knows he is doing a little bit of good.

Tell Joe and Mrs. Martin and Frances I said "Hello." I'll drop them a card soon.

We sure have a bunch of good fellows here in our barracks. We have a swell time. One fellow got a 5 lb. box of fancy cookies today from home and we all had some of them. Then every night we take turns standing in front of a long mirror and someone gives out commands and we perform and iron out the rough spots.

Well I've got to close and get ready for bed. Tomorrow we get lectures on military censorship and enemy Information. So I'll write again as soon as I can. Don't worry about me and don't forget the soap please.

LOTS OF LOVE,
HARRY JR.

Wednesday Night
8:45 P.M.

Hi Mom & Dad:

I am still okay. I really am getting tan. I just got done taking a shower, shaving and brushing my teeth. I also just finished looking at Monday's *Times-Gazette*. Drushel gets it then I get it from him.

Thanks a lot for the money belt, $2.00 and the letter Pop. I bet that is the first letter of that kind that you have written in a long time. I think the last time I got mail from you was when you were in Atlantic City with the Ford Motor Co. You and John didn't do so hot in golf did you? I suppose it was the first time this year. There is a golf course around here some place but I haven't seen it yet. I'll bet it is really up hill and down. I haven't got a road map yet. The next time I go in town I can get one at a filling station. I know we are exactly 5 miles directly east of Spartansburg. It is on any U.S. map.

Don't worry about me loaning any money. I still have $17.00 and the $2.00 that you sent. I haven't played any cards since I have been here at Camp Croft. I played some pedro at Ft. Ben but there wasn't any money in it.

They kept Herman Luteman at Ft. Ben for a while. He had to play in the band for some kind of a show and parade. But I saw in Monday's *T. G.* that he is now in Virginia. He went to a chemical warfare corp. Drushel is a truck driver and so are Donald Fowler and a fellow by the name of Goon. They are all from Ashland and they sleep in the 2nd Platoon next to mine.

Junior Jenkins (Charlie Jenkins' boy) is in the 4th Platoon. He is going to be an armor artificer or in other words a gunsmith and also repair field artillery pieces. Raymond Clark is a straight infantryman. He is on the other side of camp and I haven't seen him since the day we got here.

That sure was too bad about Bill Shinn. He lived right beside the Ashland Theater I think.

I am going to the dentist at 12:15 tomorrow so I'll get all fixed up and it will be on Uncle Sam.

Mom, I don't need any P. & G. soap. We have plenty of G.I. soap here and it sure is good stuff. I am doing my own laundry. It would cost only $1.50 a month but I can drive home on the money I can save by just doing my own wash for 16 or 17 weeks.

Today we practiced throwing dummy hand grenades. Then we also were taught how to fall forward while charging with our rifles. We also had to crawl and creep. The dust was about 2 inches thick. We sure were dirty when we got done. We had to lay flat on our belly with our head on one side and our rifles laying across our arms, which are out in front and crawl for 75 yards. You can't raise up or nothing. They sure put us through hell and high water. But it has to be done. The first thing after breakfast we marched for 4 1/2 miles with packs and rifles. I am the pacesetter for the 3rd Platoon. I march 3 or 4 paces in front of the rest and on the right. I set a pace at either 108 steps a minute or up to 120 steps a minute, whatever the 2nd lieutenant orders. After about 15 minutes marching I can tell what pace I am at.

I got a letter from Kay today and one from Rose and Wick, and one from you folks and the money belt and a paper from the church in Mansfield.

Well I've got to close now and go to sleep. If you find anything good to eat up there don't forget I'm down here. Write as soon as you can.

LOVE, HARRY JR.

Mom and Dad

Dad was parts manager at the local Ford dealership – the garage mentioned in the letters. Mom was a sales clerk at J.C. Penney's.

Sunday 1:45 P.M.
5/28/44

Dear Mom & Dad:

Well, I received a letter from you this morning and sure was glad to hear from you. I also got a letter from Inez and a box of "Sutters Taffy" from Kay and a letter from the Mansfield Tire. The Tire sent me two checks. One was for $15.34, refund on income tax for the month of April, and the other was for $22.00 refund on bond money I had accumulated. I signed them both and sent them on to Kay.

Well, Mom you asked me a lot of questions in your letter so I'll try and answer them all now. This army life is okay. It is getting tougher and rougher every day but you get used to it. As long as a fellow gets mail from home he can stand all kinds of hell and not even bat an eye. It is really hot here. I sweat a lot and I don't mind it. That was Harry Robertson's brother that had his hand taken off. He used to be a Western Union boy. That sure is too bad.

I have gotten letters from you, Kay, Inez and Rose and Wick. It keeps me busy writing but it passes away the time and I can always write a card if I can't a letter.

I suppose when you get your vacation Martha Kay will be a permanent fixture around your house for 2 weeks. I sent her a box of candy today. It had in it 3 or 4 candy bars, a pack of gum, 2 boxes of Cracker Jack, a pair of crossed rifles and some pictures of camp. I hope she will like it.

I got the money belt and soap okay. Thanks for sending it.

Drushel, Jenkins and I went to chapel this morning. It started at 9 and was out at 10. You ought to see the organ they've got. It is small like a studio piano but it is electric and it sure sounds nice. It has all the stops on it just like that big one at the Trinity Lutheran Church.

The chaplain is a nice man. He is back from overseas duty. I imagine he is around 50 years old. When the corporal played that special music a lot of men who have returned from overseas duty had to wipe away the tears. It really was a very nice service. We are going next Sunday unless we get a special detail or something.

I'll appreciate anything that you send me. I get awful hungry for something that would come from up home.

Kay sends the *News Journal* to me and Drushel gets the *Times Gazette* so we swap papers and that way we get to read them all. I just got done reading Thursday's and Friday's papers.

I haven't weighed myself for a week now so I don't know how much I weigh. We took a 3-mile hike Friday night. It was just like walking around the block to me. That is one thing I can be thankful for that I have good feet.

Last night (Saturday night) I washed 6 handkerchiefs, 3 pair of sox, 4 undershirts and 3 pair of shorts, 2 towels, 12 wash clothes and 1 fatigue shirt and 1 pair of fatigue pants. Not a bad wash for me.

Well I've got to close and write to Kay. Write when you can and I'll answer as quick as I can.

LOVE, HARRY JR.

Saturday Night
8:30 P.M.

Hi Pop:

How's things with you? Okay I hope. I got your letter Wednesday or Thursday and I just got time to answer it now. It is Saturday night. I just came back from the main post exchange. Two of my buddies and myself went up and drank 3 bottles of Budweiser beer & then came back to the barracks. It poured down rain here for about an hour and I mean it really came down. That is the second rain since we have been here.

Well next week we start our 4th week and the last week of "dry run." Starting the 5th week we use live ammunition and everything is for real. This next week we learn how to aim and fire our rifles without bullets. We had our regular Saturday inspection this afternoon. My rifle passed okay except for the hinge on the bottom of the butt plate where we keep our cleaning tools. It had a couple grains of sand on it but the 2nd lieutenant just showed it to me and told me to get it cleaned out. Boy, he sure grabs that rifle out of our hands. When I see his right arm start up to grab my rifle I just let it drop and stand as stiff as possible. Our sergeant tells us not to breathe unless it is absolutely necessary. Some of the fellows had to stay in the barracks tonight for not having clean rifles and bayonets.

I got another typhoid shot in my right arm this afternoon. That is 3 shots and 1 vaccination so far. My vaccination took okay but it didn't get sore like the one did when I was in school.

It sure is hot here now. Friday it was 105 and today 102. All we get done is crawling in the sand and sweating. I sweat clear through my fatigue shirt and when we creep on our backs my shirt has mud on it. We have to go through barbed wire on our back and they sure eat you up if you touch any of it. The other day we all had to dig foxholes 2 ft. wide, 3 1/2 ft. long and 5 1/2 ft. deep and in this red clay it sure is tough. Well, we got them all dug and then they told us to fill them back in. They didn't even come around to inspect them first. Boy, did we bitch. Sergeant Clark said that's one thing a soldier could do was bitch and we sure get plenty of it done.

Send me cake, cookies, olives, pickles, cheese, crackers or anything like that. We don't get any of those extra things here so whatever you can find will be okay I'm sure.

Did Smitty pass his exam up in Cleveland? If he ever gets in here they'll kill him. He is too heavy to march and drill like we do. I sure am glad I'm not too heavy. I weigh 144 now. I weighed 137 1/2 when I left home I think. Is Hugo a first or second lieutenant? I sure would like to see him. I suppose he will be going across pretty soon.

Yes, I sleep good at night. It cools off to about 70 at night and I sleep with just a sheet on me.

I don't know how long I'll be pace setter for our platoon. They like to switch around but as yet I'm still in front. We get 2 hikes a week. They are around 6 miles apiece. Just like walking around the block to me now. In our 15th week we get a 20-mile hike so we have got something to look forward to.

We get K.P. here about once every month or so. It is sure hell. I'd sooner crawl on my belly all day than do that. All you do is sweep and scrub and sweep and scrub and then you change and scrub and sweep. I put in 18 hours I think the day I was on.

Drushel drills everyday and does the same things as I do. When our 7 weeks are up he will go to motor mechanics school and I'll go to cook school. He isn't so much in love with this life. They are cutting his waistline down some and the morning exercises sort of get him down. The day it was 105 here 17 fellows passed out taking exercises. These salt tablets help me out a lot. They make you sweat and keep you from getting thirsty.

Well I've got to close now and go to sleep. Write when you can. Tell Dale and John and Sim I said Hello. How's the whiskey business? I'd give a lot for a shot now. Don't forget to let Mom read this too.

LOVE, HARRY JR.

Sunday Morning
10:15 A.M.

Dear Mom & Dad:

Hello folks, how are you both feeling? I am still okay. I just came from church. We had communion this morning.

First I want to thank you both for the boxes you sent to me. They sure hit the spot. I am saving Pop's box for next week. That cheese and pickles and olives will taste awful good after being on the rifle range all day. Also thanks for the $2 Pop. I've got money all right but a couple of dollars keeps me from breaking $5s or $10s or $20s. And believe it or not I've got a brand new $20 hid away along with two new $5s. That 2 bucks will buy me beer, candy, writing paper and whatever I need for a week. Say, if you ever run onto a real good toothbrush in town there please buy it for me. The best I can get here is a 25 cent one, it isn't bad but they get soft too quick. I've got two of them and I change over every day.

Pop, some Ashland fellows here say you can get tires in West Salem. They will *lend* them to you. Maybe you can get in on that.

We had a big time the night of the invasion. We woke up at 3 o'clock in the morning and listened to the radio until reveille at 5:40. This coming Thursday we have open house here. Demonstrating, drilling, rifle shooting, hand grenade, field artillery and everything that is in the infantry. I believe it is a nationwide celebration in honor of the infantryman.

Tomorrow morning we get up a 4 o'clock and eat breakfast at 4:40 and leave for the range at 5:35. We eat dinner on the range and get back to camp around 4 or 5 o'clock in the evening. We have 7 miles to walk out to the range and 7 miles back. We do this for one week. I imagine next Sunday will be a welcome day of rest. We have to make a 140 out of a possible 210 to qualify. I'll get along okay. I never did any shooting at home and it wasn't hard for me to learn the army way of shooting. Some fellows sure are having a time trying to change from their style of firing to the army way. Even left-handed shooters have to shoot right-handed.

There is a powerful big crap game going on about 10 feet in front of me! One fellow made $135 from Friday night until now and he is still going strong.

I passed rifle inspection and field equipment inspection on top yesterday. Friday night we left here at 7:30 and went on a hike. We got way out in the country and then we were divided up into squads and then we tried to capture each other. It was darker than hell and we crawled, crept, run and jumped over high grass, through woods, creeks, brush and what have you. Then to top it all off we had a nice hard rain about 10 o'clock. I got my raincoat out of my pack in time to keep from drowning. My poor rifle was soaking wet from rain and red clay. We got back to camp at midnight and we ate some coffee and donuts. Then I stayed up and shit, showered and shaved and then went to work on my rifle. I got to bed at 15 till 2. We were allowed to sleep till 6:30, then we ate breakfast and got ready for inspection. After dinner we had a class on patrol missions and then a picture on "Why We Fight."

Last night was Saturday night and again I stayed away from town. Some of us went up to our company beer garden and drank some beer and then we came back to the barrack and shot the bull and I wrote a letter to Kay.

I'm sending Martha Kay another box this afternoon, candy and Cracker Jack and gum. I know she likes it and there isn't anything else here to get her.

Well, I've got to close and go eat my Sunday chicken dinner. Tell Kay to show you my test paper that has a superior rating on it by Major Grey. Also my teeth are classified as "excellent." So I'm going to keep them that way. I got another tetanus shot in my right arm yesterday. Not sore a bit. It stung for a half hour but was okay after that. Write when you can and I sure appreciate the food that you sent. I'll write as soon as I can again. Once a week is about all I can make so far and so I try to make it as long and interesting as possible.

LOVE, HARRY JR.

Tell everyone I said "Hello."

"Two Harrys" said my mother Martha.

Sunday Afternoon
June 25, 1944

Dear Mom and Dad:

Hello again. How are you two by now? I am still okay. I weighed 152 lbs. Friday night. So you can see the army isn't hurting me.

I guess I neglected you folks last week. I didn't have much time to write. I wrote to Kay everyday but Friday or Thursday. We were on the rifle range Thursday until about 3:30 in the afternoon and then we had to change clothes and be ready for a parade at 4:10. We got done parading at 6:15 and then we had to change clothes and roll full field packs and be ready to go on a "shuttle" hike at 7:30. In a shuttle hike you walk part way and then ride in trucks part way. We walked 13 miles and rode 15 miles, a total of 28 miles. We got back at 12:30 midnight and went right to bed. We were all wore out. Some fellows had some awful bad feet. I had a small blister on my right big toe. It is gone now so I'm okay.

I got your box Thursday but didn't open it until Friday noon. Everything was okay. It just hits the spot. I got a box from the Mansfield Tire Friday night. It had a tube of toothpaste in it, 2 tubes of Barbasol shaving cream, 1 package of razor blades, 2 large Nestles chocolate bars, 1 box of peanut butter candy, 1 box of candied fruits, 1 box of cookies and 1 box of hard candy. It was real nice.

Well I start to cook school a week from Monday. When we get transferred to another camp we will get T-4 or T-5 rating.

The T-4 receives a sergeant's pay and the T-5 gets a corporal's pay.

The stripes look like this; you've seen a lot of them on soldiers I know. The T-4 and T-5 both have the same kind of stripes.

Tomorrow we start on our 7th week and it is the finishing touches of our basic training. Then we get 8 weeks of school and then in our 15 and 16th weeks we go out on maneuvers. And in our 17th week we get rested up and have a few parties and get ready to check out for places unknown.

I got a letter from John and Inez today. Inez said Chuck Grimm arrived in England. He is going to get his crack at Germany I suppose. I imagine he is satisfied now.

We have all decided here at camp that if we get a chance to capture Hitler or Tojo we won't kill them right then. First we are going to bring them back to Camp Croft and make them take basic training like we had to. If they are still alive then it is hard to tell what would happen.

New fellows come into camp here every week. I sure pity the ones that have those 7 weeks to go through in July and August. I doubt if I could take it again. This heat is tough but I'm used to it now. If I can walk with steel helmet, full field pack and rifle and rifle belt in temperatures from 90 to 106 I guess I can stand anything else that might come on. I'm glad now that I volunteered when I did. I'm just about 4 or 6 weeks ahead of the bunch I would have left with. From here on in it is going to be chicken.

That toothbrush was just right. It sure is a dandy. I've got 4 now. That way they can't get soft on me. I change about, using one every 4 days. I'll need some more Lifebouy soap soon so when you get the time you can send me 3 or 4 bars.

About that target practice, Pop, I sure have had plenty, one whole week of rapid and slow fire at 200, 300 and 500 yards. That was when I qualified as a marksman. Last week we fired .22 rifles. Compared to our Garand M-1 rifles the .22 is like a cap gun. Our M-1 is semi-automatic and holds a clip of 8 rounds and the bullet travels 2,700 feet per second. When we first fired it we all slid back about 3 or 4 inches from the kick but the secret to that is to keep your sling as tight as you can stand it. That way it can't jump out of your shoulder. The chamber pressure is 54,000 lbs. per square inch so you can see it sure has power.

Last week we fired at moving targets, with .22 rifles. They used model airplanes and trucks and tanks. Tomorrow morning we fire our M-1 at moving figures of men and tanks. Tuesday we fire a 50 caliber heavy machine gun and maybe a bazooka.

Mom, I'll bet you and Martha Kay had a good time together. I wish she could have gone to the carnival but there will be plenty more chances for her to go.

The only person at church that I have received any mail from is Mrs. Clauser up at Savannah. I can't place her but she did write a nice letter and I've got to answer it too as soon as I can.

Yes, I know that Mr. Wise. His wife is a Parker. They used to deal at Zehners. They lived on Union Street and I used to deliver groceries to them. They've got 3 or 4 children I think. I think he worked at Myers. He'll get more money in the army than he did at home I bet.

Junior Jenkins and Drushel are okay. Their wives will be here the first of July I think. Drushel passed out one day when we came back from the range. He marched back okay, but when he sat down on his locker in front of his bed he just dropped over. Lieutenant Morrison worked on him and finally brought him to.

I went to town last night and danced at the U.S.O. I met a Lieutenant Sarah Anderson from Wooster, Ohio. She is a Lieutenant in the Army Nurse Corp. She was just as glad to talk to me about Wooster and Ashland and Mansfield as I was to her. I showed her Kay and Martha Kay's picture and she wants to meet Kay when she comes down if she can. I danced a couple dances with her and one with a WAC and a couple with some other girls. The dance was over at 11:30 and the other 2 fellows and I went and ate some hamburgs and then came back to camp.

Well I've got to close. I've run off enough here for one day. Write again when you can. Pop, how did you manage to write me 4 pages in that letter? It was swell. Keep it up.

LOVE, HARRY JR.

Sunday Morn.
10:30 A.M.

Dear Mom and Dad:

Hi folks, how are you? I am okay. I have a new address now. It is Co. D, 27th I.T.B. 3rd Pltn. Don't forget to change it now.

We moved Saturday afternoon. This whole company is cooks. We start to school tomorrow morning. Drushel is in my old barracks now, Co. A, 28th 3rd Pltn. and Jenkins moved to Co. D, 28th, 1st Pltn. I am just across the street from my old barracks.

Well it rained here last night and it is cloudy today and pretty cool. I just came from church at 10 o'clock. I got up at 7 this morning. We had breakfast at 7:30. It sure is a lot nicer here in Co. D than it was in A-28. In A-28 we ate cafeteria style and there was a lot of noise and here we eat family style. The food is set on our table in big plates and when the plate is empty the table waiter fills it up again. It is just like eating at home now.

Well this week ended our basic training. We were out on the range again and we fired 30 and 50 calibre machine guns and bazookas and 30 calibre carbines. Those machine guns are sure nice to fire. We had stationary tanks for targets. The bazooka was interesting too. It doesn't kick at all. It has a back flash of fire of about 10 or 12 feet and it is fired by dry cell batteries. Then Friday we fired the carbine. It sure is light. It is easier than a .22 to fire. I had a good score on it. 180 out of 200. That is not bad.

My job as pacemaker is over now. We will only hike once a week and I suppose somebody else will get a chance at it now.

I saw in the *Times Gaz.* where 2 Mexicans were going to sing out at the park.

Well I sure am getting anxious to see Kay. I am going to call her up at your house Sunday the 9th. I will have her room address then for her and she can go right there from the bus station. And if we don't go on a hike Friday night I can go in and see her and if we do hike I'll have to wait and see her Saturday. I guess Drushel's and Jenkins's wives got here yesterday okay. I haven't seen them yet but I know they were to get here at 4:22 the same time Kay will get here.

I am going to a show tonight. It is Pat O'Brian in "Marine Raiders."

You tell John and Inez about my change of address too.

Well I can't think of anything more to write so I'll close and hope to hear from you soon. Thanks again for the box. I've got some cheese and pickles left and also one box of sardines. Write when you can.

LOVE, HARRY JR.

This is a post card I got at Camp Croft and is just like the mess hall I ate in. Those black stoves were not needed while I was there, it was hot enough and there was no air conditioning in those days.

Sunday 1:00 P.M.

Hi Mom and Pop:

I just got done talking to you on the phone and now I'll try and explain a few things to you about this cook school.

First of all we had a rifle inspection Saturday afternoon and I had the best rifle in the whole platoon. The bore of my rifle actually sparkled. Lieutenant Katz said that he could see that I had put a lot of work on it and that I was really trying hard. He told the rest of the platoon that they should look at my rifle and use it for an example to go by. After he dismissed us he called me over and said "Hamilton, is your wife in town?" I said "No, sir, but she'll be here next Friday and I want to get her room for her tonight." He said he thought there was something in back of it all. He told me if I had been on guard duty I would have been selected as the colonel's orderly. All that the colonel's orderly has to do is report to the colonel's quarters at 8 o'clock in the morning and then he is off the rest of the day and he also gets a 24 hours pass whenever he wants it. Well, so much for that.

We were issued our white uniforms yesterday; 2 caps, 2 coats, 2 trousers, 3 aprons. Thursday afternoon we had our blood tested and we will get food handler certificates sometime this week. I think for this week we will cook 3 hours a day. The class is divided into 2 groups, A and B. I am in group B. This week group A will go to work from 4 in the morning until 7 and group B will take over from 7 till 10. Then we have 5 hours of school after that. We change about each day. Monday we go to work at 7 in the morning and Tuesday we go in at 4. Then week after next we will work this way: I will go to work at 4 in the morning and off at noon and then back to work at noon the next day until 7 or 8 o'clock at night. Then back in at 4 in the morning until noon and then off till noon the next day again. As student cooks we do not have to work on Sundays. We have 1 hour a day of physical exercise. We all will be fat as pigs by the time our 17 weeks are done. Well we keep up that schedule until our 15th week and then we go out on maneuvers for our 15th and 16th weeks. Then we cook for about 400 to 500 men. We take turns in being mess sergeants, 1st cooks, 2nd cooks and 3rd cooks and of course we will have K.P. duty too. We work the same hours when we cook but when we get K.P. we are on it all day.

This week we have been taking notes in our notebooks and I've got 30 pages on both sides. Friday morning we baked oatmeal cookies, 72 dozen of them for Co. D mess hall and in the afternoon we baked devils food cake for 300 men. Saturday we were shown how the army cuts beef up. They never use a saw. Just a boning knife and butcher knife and a meat hook.

Last night I was in town and drank a couple quarts of Red Top beer from Cincinnati, Ohio. They have Blatz beer at our Post Exchange and beer garden. I was talking to the man who runs the P.X. and he showed me some records of June's business. They did a little over $28,000 business in June. And they sell 16 to 20 barrels of beer a day. That is just for one P.X. and there are 5 more like it plus the Main P.X. here. Pretty good business isn't it.

Drushel was on guard duty last Wednesday night. He didn't like it at all. He is in the platoon I moved out of in the 28th. I made a sketch of my surroundings so you can see what's what.

A bunch of new fellows came in last night. I can just imagine what is going through their minds. They came from Ft. Devens, Massachusetts. There was a bunch came in from Ft. Ben in Indiana. The train had a wreck in Jellico, Tennessee and 40 of them were killed and 100 and some injured. One of the ones that were killed was from Columbus and one from Massillon.

I have been feeling so good lately that I can hardly believe it myself. We are getting a lot of hand to hand combat training and the art of Jiu Jitsu. We get that in our hour of physical training. I can throw a person down without using my hands, only my feet. We are trained how to break out of a choking grip or how to stop a right or left jab and apply a very painful hold after we stop it. You don't have to be big to get a man down. Just be fast and he'll go down every time. We get into sawdust pits and practice with each other and we take on each other, big or small. And the most important thing they teach us is to protect ourselves from a blow in our privates. But we are taught how to and when to apply that blow also.

Well I got Kay a nice room in town. It is in a big home and the people are very nice. Well, I've got to close now. I can't think of anything more to write. Thanks a lot for the box and stationery. Don't send anything now until I write for it. I'll be working in the kitchen and I'll keep plenty full and we are getting fed so much better here in the 27th than we did in the 28th. The mess sergeant even comes around and asks us if we had enough. Write when you can and I'll let you know if anything new comes up.

LOVE, HARRY JR.

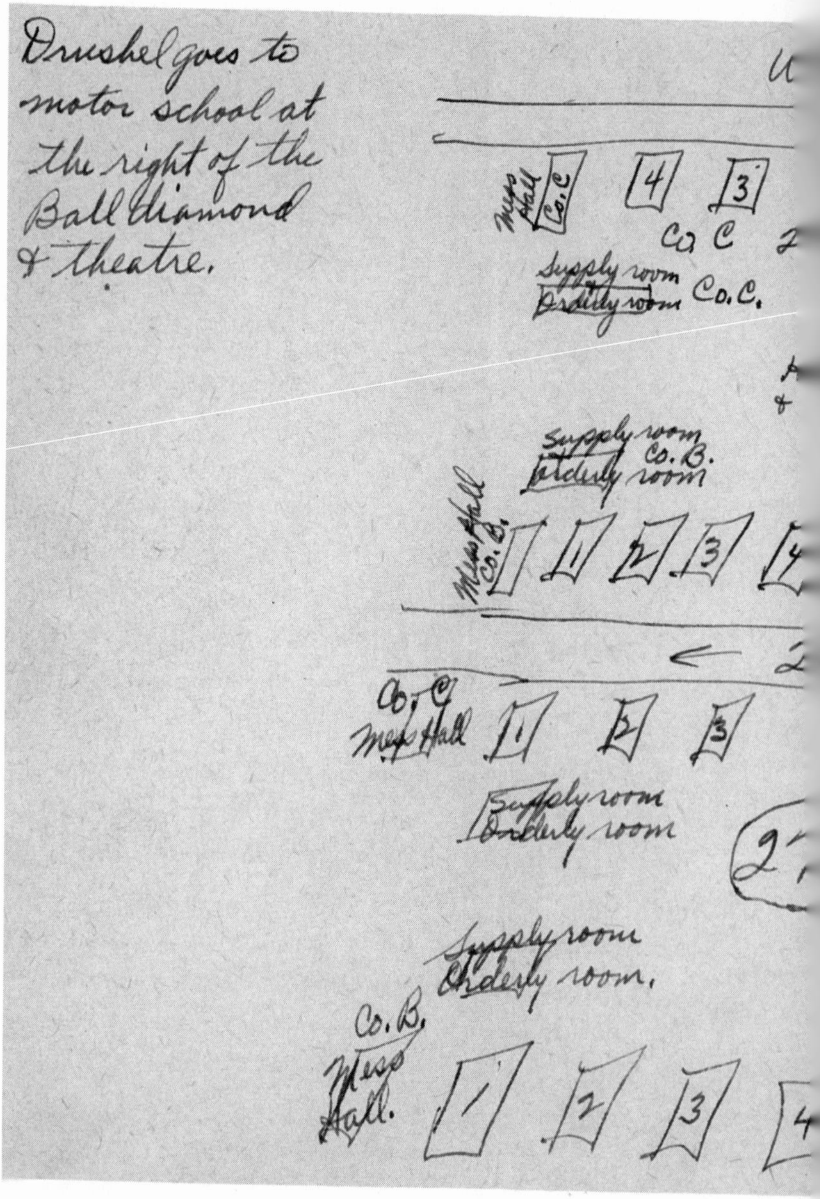

Drushel goes to
motor school at
the right of the
Ball diamond
& theatre.

Mess Hall | Co. C | [4] | [3]

Co C

Supply room
Orderly room | Co. C.

Supply room
Co. B.
Orderly room

Mess Hall
Co. B. | [1] | [2] | [3] | [4]

Co. C
Mess Hall | [1] | [2] | [3]

Supply room
Orderly room

Supply room
Orderly room.

Co. B.
Mess
Hall. | [1] | [2] | [3] | [4]

Beer garden here | Ball diamond

3th Street → | Theatreps here

[1] [4] [3] [2] [1] [Mess Hall C.O] | [ ] Infirmary

platoons Co. D 28th Bn.
Jr. Jenkins is here.

th Bn.

Co D → Supply room / ~~Orderly room~~

whes I was
l is there now

Co A. Supply room / orderly room
Druskel used to be here.

Jenkins
was here

[4 Pltn] [3 Pltn] [2 Pltn] [Pltn] [Co. A Mess Hall] | 28th Bn. Recreation Hall.

Street → | Post Exchange

Jenkins goes to School here ↓

[4 Pltn] [3 Pltn] [2 Pltn] [Pltn] [Co. D Mess Hall 27th] | Armor Artificer School

Co. D 27th Bn.

Bn) I am here now | Guard House

ket ball court Horseshoe Court Co. D Supply room / orderly room | 27th Bn. Recreation Hall

Co A. Supply room / orderly room

[4] [3] [2] [1] [Co. A mess Hall] | Cook school across street. 2 bldgs. look ↑

Sunday Noon

Dear Mom and Dad:

Well here it is Sunday and I'm trying to catch up on my writing to you folks and John and Inez and a few more people. We have made a great change over here since Friday night. Starting tomorrow morning the 26th, 27th, 28th and 29th battalions or the whole 8th regiment will be straight rifle companies. In other words I'm done cooking. They are closing the cooks school and the motor mechanics and chauffeurs school and the pioneers school and all of the specialists schools. It looks like this war is going to end pretty soon if they don't need any more specialists. This change also includes Drushel and Jenkins. We are getting a break though, our class doesn't have to go back any or lose any time. We start our 13th week this Monday or tomorrow. Some of the other classes 52 and 53 have to go back to their 5th week and start over and the 5th week is range week and I sure pity them. Of course it is not going to be any snap for us either. We will get training now just like we did in our first 7 weeks only it will be more thoroughly explained and we will learn more about the machine gun and the mortar and bayonet and the Browning Automatic Rifle. We all are glad for the change. We have had a good vacation from our 7th week until our 13th. Now we will be able to take better care of ourselves if the time should come that we would go into combat. We also are glad for the change because we now will be shipped out all together and kept together as a rifle company. When we leave Camp Croft we will still be classified as having a 0-6-0 training or a specialists training and if they need cooks at any camp here or overseas we will be eligible to fill that opening or also to fill an opening as a rifleman.

I did a wonderful job of shooting the other day, Friday, on the range. We were divided into squads and were sent out on patrol or scouting missions after the supposed to be enemy. A squad has 12 men in it and each man has a certain job to do. The #1 man is the squad leader and #2 man is the right flank scout and #3 man is the left flank scout, #4 man is the BAR man (Browning Automatic Rifleman) and #5 man is the assistant BAR man and #6 is the ammunition bearer for the #4 man. #7 and 8 are right flank rifleman and #9 and 10 are left flank riflemen and #11 is the assistant squad leader and #12 is the grenadier. I was the #4 man (BAR man) and we had to crawl up to a firing line and fire at targets. My job was to fire at the surprise target that was brought up. Out of 80 shots I had 73 hits.

I was in town a while last night and I ran into Raymond Clark. It was the first I had seen him since the day we got here. His wife was here and she went back the day after Kay did. He is okay and is anxious to get home as I am. He said that John Sauder was hurt pretty bad when he was on the obstacle course one day and he will have to be in the hospital for 2 or 3 months. He is in some camp in Georgia.

Drushel is okay but he sure hates to change over to a rifle company but there is nothing he can do about it. Did Shorty Smith have to leave for the army yet? I got the $3 okay and thanks a lot. I bought a 100% wool garrison cap the other day from our mess sergeant, which was $5.00 so I will be a little, short this month. In town those hats cost $8 and $9 so I did get a good buy. I've got to get some toilet articles ready for maneuvers also.

If you want to you can send me another box. Since I will be out of the kitchen now I will be able to eat more of the things that you send me. See if you can find a small box of Ritz crackers to send along. Say, do either one of you need anything? I can get a lot of drugs and powders and flashlight batteries and things like that. If there is something you can't find at home let me know and I'll see if I can get it. I can buy cigarettes for $1.20 a carton.

Well, I'm going to close and start a letter to John and Inez. So write when you can.

LOVE, HARRY JR.

Taken during Kay's 10 day visit to Camp Croft. She traveled by bus for a day and a half and stayed with a family that rented out 4 rooms in their home to wives of soldiers that came to visit.

Sunday Afternoon

Hi Mom and Dad:

Well, here it is Sunday and I'm tired and aching and have an awful sore right knee. As you know we went through the battle courses Friday and Saturday and it sure was something to talk about. We used live ammunition all of the time and we sure learned a lot on how to handle it. We also threw live grenades and shot a grenade launcher. Our Sargeant, Sargeant Clark, was seriously wounded Friday morning. He was in the hand grenade pits and he was to show the trainee how to throw the grenade from the pit into some foxholes. Some trainee from Drushel's platoon pulled the pin on the grenade and then got excited and dropped it. Sargeant Clark shoved him out of the way and fell on the grenade. He got two shrapnel wounds in his shoulder and one in his head. He is still unconscious and they have given him plasma 3 times and scraped the bone or skull a couple of times too. We sure hope he comes through okay.

Saturday afternoon we went through the machine gun fire and barbed wire and we did it Saturday night also. I made a drawing of the course, so Pop would understand more about what we did.

The dust was about 6 inches deep on this course and we sure got dirty. The TNT charges blew up more dirt and stones and we had to bury our faces when they went off. We also threw 3 hand grenades apiece and fired at surprise targets and were on a bayonet assault course, a close combat course. And we captured a village with 60 MM mortar fire and 30 calibre machine guns, grenades and rifles. Well, so much for that.

Mom, that was Fred Koepplin that was in Indiana. He liked to drink beer and play cards. I've got to go and eat now so will close and write again this week.

LOVE, HARRY JR.

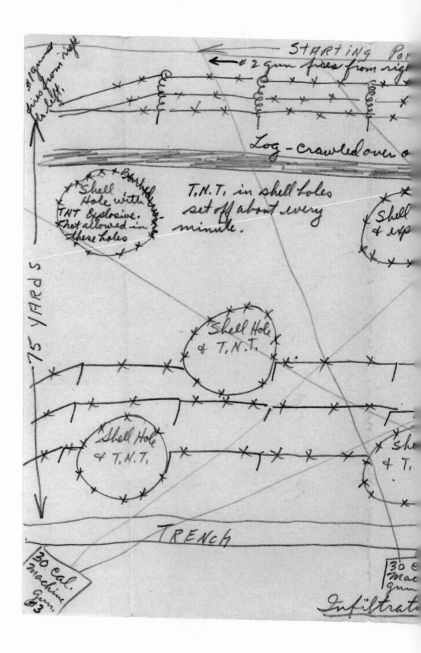

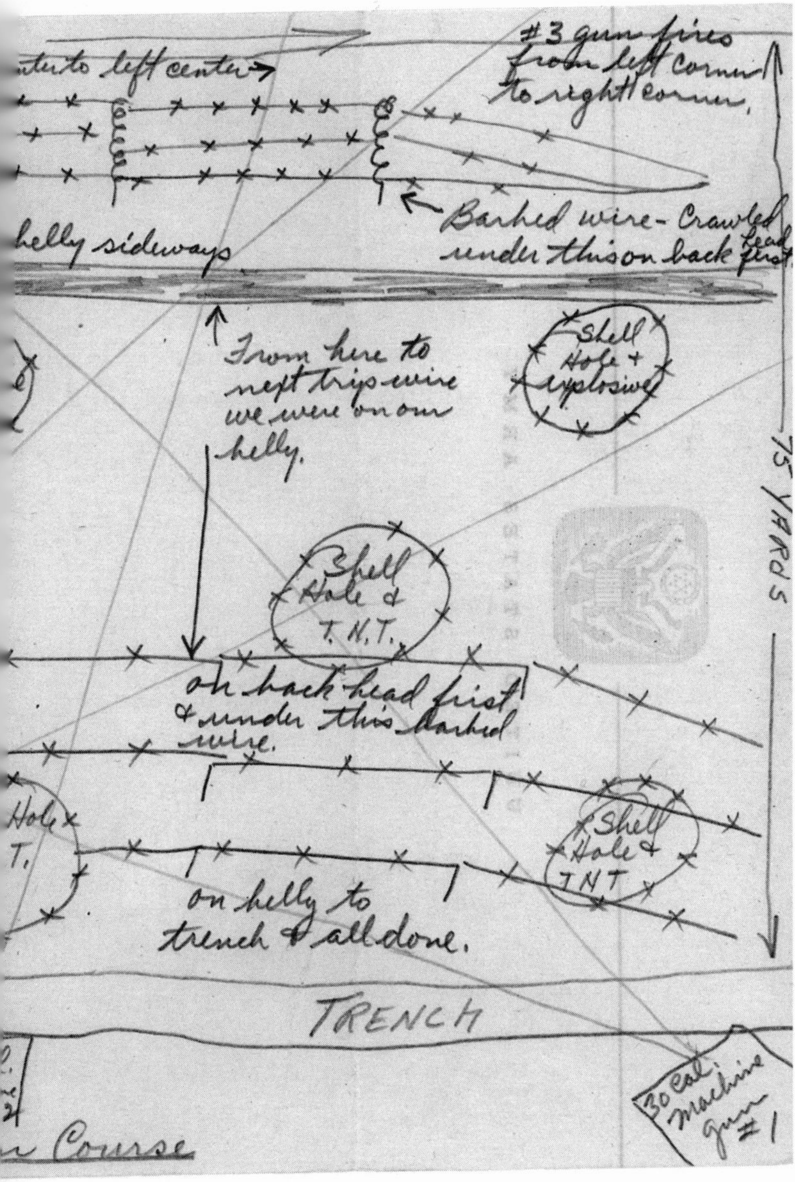

...nter to left center →

#3 gun fires
from left corner
to right corner.

← Barhed wire – Crawled
under this on back head first

belly sideways.

↑ From here to
next trip wire
we were on our
belly.

Shell
Hole &
explosive

Shell
Hole &
T.N.T.

on back head first
& under this barbed
wire.

Hole ×
T.

Shell
Hole &
TNT

on belly to
trench & all done.

TRENCH

75 YARDS

30 Cal.
machine
gun
#1

Course

Sunday Eve.

Dear Mom and Dad:

Hi folks, how are you? I am still okay. I guess I still weigh around 155 and I feel very good. My right knee is still a little sore. There is a big scab on it now and every time I bend my leg too much it cracks open and it takes a long time for it to heal up. This last week wasn't so tough. We were out on the range firing the light machine gun and we practiced firing the mortar with dummy ammunition.

Well, Sargeant Clark is improving very much. He was unconscious for 5 days.

We think that we are moving to Co. B, 27th this Thursday but we are not sure yet. Our Lieutenant Katz was transferred to the 28th and a Lieutenant Coleman is going to take his place. Wouldn't it be nice if it would be Lieutenant Carl Coleman from Ashland? I haven't seen the man yet but I don't imagine we would be that lucky to get him. I don't know if he is back from the islands yet.

Yes, I was expecting to change to a rifle company. We just found out that the cook school here isn't even recognized by the army. So we would have taken cooks training for 10 weeks and then put into a rifle company without any experience. So it is better this way. It isn't any tougher than our first 7 weeks was. We walked out to the range last Wednesday (4 and 6/10 miles) in one hour and 5 minutes with full pack and rifle and then we came back in one hour flat. We sang all the way in and didn't mind the pace. Oh yes, I was the pacesetter that day too. I was pacesetter all this week.

I got the box okay. The crackers and sandwich spread is about gone and I'm saving the sardines and cheese to take along out on maneuvers.

Well, we are about to start our 15th week and it won't be long and I'll be on my way home for a few days. So, Pop tell Shorty to fork over some gas tickets because I'm going to need them. And you might have to do a little walking too for a few days. Oh yes, I drove a jeep the other day. I had to come in and get the ammunition from the range and it sure felt good to drive again.

Well I'm going to go and shave and shower. So I'll write again in the middle of the week. Write to me when you can.

LOVE, HARRY JR.

Sunday afternoon

Dear Mom and Dad:

Hi folks. One week of maneuvers has gone by and we are starting on our 17th and last week of basic training. I don't know when I'll be home but I hope to be home by the first of the 19th week. I got your box of candy the other day and it sure was good. About 30 other fellows had at least a taste of it. We are getting good eats here but we could eat a lot more on account of being in the open all the time. I wrote and told Kay to tell you to send me more cheese and sardines but the candy was okay so just forget the other. One thing that would go good out here is a cold bottle of beer.

Last Saturday, Sunday and Monday it rained and of course we got soaked and just let our clothes on and when the sun came out Tuesday it dried us and the ground out too. Then it rained again Thursday night and Friday we dried out again. Pop, these tents here are just as good as nothing when it comes to shedding water. They were probably left over from 1918. We have been on the go night and day here. We walk from 15 to 20 miles every day and we have to have our steel helmets, gas mask, rifle and rifle belts on all the time when we eat, or even when we go to the latrine. Today we were not tactical so we don't have to wear them until 8 o'clock tonight when we have a night problem until midnight. We were out 3 nights last week until from 4 to 6 in the morning and then slept until noon and up and at it until midnight or later again. Tomorrow we move close to some town about 10 miles from here and put on a demonstration how to take or capture a hill. The heavy weapons outfit is going with us and I guess we are going to make quite a lot of noise with our rifles, machine guns and 60 m.m. mortar and their big heavy guns. I guess the general is going to be there watching also. The demonstration is Tuesday afternoon. We go back to Camp Croft at 8 o'clock Friday night. I got shorted $5.00 on my pay this time. I got $14.80 instead of my usual $19.80. About 15 of us were short and it is being looked into by our company commander for us.

I guess Camp Croft is going to train men for the Army of Occupation now and Ft. Meade, Maryland, is no longer a port of embarkation so I guess they almost know when Germany is going to fold up. I hope it is soon so we can put all of our strength in the South Seas.

Chuck Grimm got a pretty good job as an M.P. in France. It is dangerous but it is not like the front. I'll be more than willing to go over and police up the place and let the ones who did the fighting come back home. They sure deserve a rest.

Well, I've got to close now and go down to the creek and take a bath. We have running cold water but not a damn bit of hot water. I have used my steel helmet for everything but a toilet. It sure is a handy thing. Oh yes, I got the $2.00 okay. It will help for my ticket home. So I will close and hope to see you all soon.

LOVE, HARRY JR.

P.S. Every once in a while we get a snake as a bed partner early in the morning but they are too slow in waking up and we kill them before they are even awake.

Group photo taken at the end of basic training in September, 1944. After a ten day furlough we were sent on to Camp McCoy, Wisconsin for still more training while we waited to be shipped overseas. I remember a lot of 25 mile hikes with 10 minute breaks every hour.

Waiting

Monday Afternoon
4:00 P.M.

Hi Mom and Dad:

I am okay but a little chilly. It is sure cool up here and it is raining now too. It was 42 this morning. Tuesday or Wednesday we are going out on maneuvers for about 3 weeks. So you can see they aren't letting up on us at all. Drushel, Jenkins and I are all split up. Even the whole platoon that I was with in Croft is split up. We are all in different companies and regiments. We aren't settled very good yet and don't know what we are in or why. I just had a clothing check about an hour ago and I get a physical exam some time today.

We got into Chicago Sunday morning at 9:45 and got our bags about 11:30 and rode to the Union Station and got on the Streamliner Hiawatha and left at 1 o'clock and got in camp at 4:45. That Streamliner sure can travel and you feel just like you are floating.

Well I've got to close now. I'll try and write as much as I can while I'm out on maneuvers. I don't need anything yet, so you won't have to send me anything to eat until I tell you so. Just write, that will help a lot.

LOVE, HARRY JR.

Friday Afternoon
4 o'clock

Dear Mom and Dad:

I just got done writing a letter to Kay and I still have time to write a few lines to you. I am out on maneuvers now and it is not too tough. Just about like we had down south only we sleep in our foxholes and very seldom put up our tent. Sometimes we just lay our shelter half on the ground and sleep on it. It rained here yesterday but today it is nice. The sun is shining and there is a breeze blowing. We are going to stay at this spot all night so that means I sleep in this foxhole I dug after dinner. We got up at 5 o'clock this morning and started walking at 8 and would walk a while and rest a while. We got to this spot about 12 o'clock and dug in and have laid around ever since. On this problem I carry a bazooka. This problem lasts until Sunday noon. The whole division is out here and it sure is some sight.

We are not using any live ammunition, just a few dummy rounds now and then. Once in a while the fellows get captured by the red army and they are exchanged the next day at 6 o'clock in the evening. This maneuver is mostly to give the officers experience in working together as a division.

I just wrote and told Kay to have you send me a box just like you sent me down at Camp Croft. Only please include a box of Anacin tablets (aspirin) and a small tube of toothpaste. I went to the dental clinic the other day to get my teeth examined and they found 3 teeth that need small fillings and down at Croft they told me my teeth were perfect. That's the Army for you.

We get a warm breakfast and supper and we eat "K" rations for dinner. I don't know what time we will eat supper tonight but I hope it comes along soon.

Well, Pop, how's the tires holding out? I hope you can get some soon or you will be walking.

We finally found seats on the train to Chicago and I slept or tried to all the way to Chicago. I got my bags okay and then we transferred to the Union Station. We are all split up down here now and I saw Drushel twice since we got here. So far we are all riflemen but won't get classified until after maneuvers.

I haven't seen that fellow from Maine that I brought that snapshot for. I got it back in the barracks and I'll send it to you when I get back in. Send the box of food and tablets and toothpaste whenever you get a chance. Write to me both of you because mail is sure a nice thing to get out here in this wilderness. We only get mail call once every 2 or 3 days. We move so fast the mailman can't catch up with us. So I'll write again when I can and I'll be looking for your most welcome letters.

LOVE, HARRY JR.

Tuesday Night

Dear Mom and Pop:

Mom, I received your letter yesterday and Pop's today so I am going to start this letter to you both tonight and probably finish it tomorrow. I just wrote one to Kay and mailed it and it is 10 after 7 now and it is getting dark and I am sitting by the bonfire trying to write this.

Well, we are still out here in this damn woods. Remind me when I come home and if we ride in the car, not to look at any woods. But it isn't so bad though. I am getting along okay and will probably be a hard guy to keep in a house after this war is over.

We had a rest all day yesterday and had a picture show out here last night. This morning we had a platoon problem and this afternoon we had a class on map reading [CENSORED].

Pop, you asked me how our non-coms and brass were up here. They are swell. They sure do treat us nice. Down in Croft a Staff Sargeant was a big fellow, he thought, but up here a Staff Sargeant is just like a buck private only he gets more money. They want us to call them by their first or last name and not sergeant so and so.

Well here is the latest dope that they tell us. We are supposed to go overseas soon. They say that this 76th division is on the alert to go over but they have been on the alert for 2 years and still haven't left so maybe this is another false alarm. Lieutenant Bloom was talking to me Sunday night and he said it was hard to tell what would happen but he says we might go to France. We

UNITED STATES ARMY

Tues. night.

Dear Mom & Pop:

Mom, I recieved your letter yesterday and Pop's today so I am going to start this letter to you both tonight and probably finish it tomorrow. I just wrote one to Kay and mailed it & it is 10 after 7 now & it is getting dark & I am sitting by the bonfire trying to write this.

Well, we are still out here in this damn woods. Remind me when I come home, & if we ride in the car, not to look at any woods. But it isn't so bad though. I am getting along O.K. & will probably be a hard guy to keep in a house after this war is over. We had a rest all day yesterday & had a picture show out here last night. This morning we had a platoon problem & this afternoon we had a class on map reading ~~~~~~~~~~~~ ~~~~~~~~~~~~ Pop, you asked me how ~~~~~~~~~~~~~~~~~~~~~~ now. We had a very easy da~~~~~~~~~ This af~~~~~~~~~~~~~ problems & got ~~~~~~~~ 15 till 4. Bankers hours have a lot of officers and non-coms back from the South Pacific and they are going with us and the government has a law that they can't send men back to the same theater of war they were fighting in.

Wednesday Afternoon, 4 o'clock

Well I had to quit writing last night so will try to finish this letter now. We had a very easy day so far. We had physical exercise this morning and than a 3 star general talked to us and he never even mentioned going overseas. His name was General Lear. He is back from France and England and he told us some inside dope. The English say that after the war is over we will owe them a lot of money. Whenever a troopship leaves the east coast for England and if it is an English ship carrying U.S. soldiers, the English government charges the United States $86.50 per soldier to transport them across the ocean and $94.50 for the officers. Isn't that something? This general was with the troops that made the invasion on Cherbourg, France, from England and he said that the U.S. was charged so much per man to transport them on English ships across the channel. He said there would be a lot of arguments on who owes who when this is over.

This afternoon [CENSORED] problems and got done about 15 till 4. Bankers hours don't you think? We are done now till we get up at 6:30 in the morning.

I got a letter from Inez and John and also the papers you sent and also a box of candy from Kay. Those papers sure look good, you save them each week and send them to me please.

I've got to close now and get ready to eat supper. Write when you can and I will too.

LOVE, HARRY JR.

P.S. Pop, there is no one here in this bunch from home. One fellow named Nelson is from Cleveland and another from Dayton called Adams.

Family photo taken while on furlough in September, 1944

Monday P.M.

Dear Mom and Dad:

Hi folks. Here it is Monday and we are sitting around here in the barracks doing nothing. I have already written a letter to Kay and one to John and Inez and I'll start on yours now.

Well a lot has happened since I wrote to you last. First we had our maneuvers cut short 2 weeks and last night the captain had our company assemble in the mess hall and he told us that we are going overseas and that we will have very few weekends to spend here at Camp McCoy. All men who are on furlough have been sent telegrams to report back at once and no one is allowed out of camp and no one is allowed to come in to camp and no one is allowed to make any long distance phone calls and all division identification has to be off of our clothes such as shoulder patches and pins on our caps and stuff like that, so when some one sees a trainload of soldiers going through they won't know what outfit they are from.

Pop, here is a leak in telling us where we are going. We are going to carry these old rifles and gas masks with us. Unless we get them exchanged for new ones at our port of embarkation we surely aren't going into a combat area with those things. That leads me to believe that we are going to France or Germany as the Army of Occupation or else we are going to Alaska or Africa or somewhere where there is very little fighting going on. This is the first time a whole division has moved out with their old rifles and gas masks. The captain says that he can't understand it either so I guess we will just sit and wait and see what will happen.

Well, so much for that. I'll let you know if something hot comes up. I already wrote and told Kay about it so you don't have to be afraid of telling her something I wouldn't want her to know.

I got your box of food last week and we ate it in about an hour and I also got the small box yesterday. Thanks a lot, they sure did come in handy, Yes, by all means keep on sending the papers to me. They sure look good up here. We even put them inside of our jackets to help keep us warm.

I haven't had my other 2 teeth filled yet. They don't bother me at all and I can't find any spots on them. I think it was a peanut hull that the dentist saw instead of a spot on my teeth. But they will fix them up for me if there is something wrong.

I am going to pack some extra clothes and things that I have accumulated and send them home because I will only be allowed so much baggage when we do leave camp.

I can't think of anything I need. I want to buy something for Kay's birthday (November 13) and send to her but I'll be darned if I know what to get. Mom, if you see any real nice dresses at the store that will fit Kay, put it back for me and let me know how much it is and I'll send the money right away, and I mean let me know how much it costs because I've got the money and I want to buy her something all by myself. I'll depend on you doing that for me now. Pick out a dress or skirt and blouse or underclothes or whatever you can find. Don't go over $15.00 though. I can afford that but it will be a little hard to go higher. I imagine you can get something pretty nice for $10.00 or so. Write and let me know what you find as soon as you can.

Well, I've got to close now. I'll let you know the latest news up here as quick as I can. Write when you can and I will too.

LOVE, HARRY JR.

P.S. Mom, don't get all worked up about my leaving here. The last time this bunch started over, half of them were on the boat and they all got called back. Maybe that won't happen this time but I'm not worried in the least about it so just take it as it comes and the best will happen to us all, I'm sure.

11:00 A.M.
Thursday

Dear Mom and Dad:

I received both of your letters yesterday and I'll probably get the papers today. We haven't done very much up here. Yesterday morning I was in a close combat problem and in the afternoon I had to throw some more live hand grenades. Last night we had a night problem from 7:30 to 11:30, all about patrolling and scouting. I sure was tired and glad to get to bed when it was over. This morning we went through a tear gas chamber and a chlorine gas chamber. I don't know what we'll do this afternoon yet.

So far I haven't heard any more about shipping out of here. They told us the other day that anybody who had cameras would be allowed to take them along. That sure sounds funny doesn't it?

As far as me getting out on account of my nerves I don't know if that will happen to me or not. I do get pretty nervous at times, especially when they don't know what they are doing but I get over it okay. Maybe if I ever see and do some of the things that those fellows across are seeing and doing I will fold up but I sure hope not.

That was sure a nice letter from Martha Kay. I am going to write her a few lines tonight and mail it to her personally. I know she gets a kick out of writing and I sure get a kick out of reading her little letters.

Well folks I haven't any more to say right now. So I'll close and try and write this week again.

LOVE, HARRY JR.

Sunday P.M.

Dear Mom and Dad:

I am at the U.S.O. in Sparta. We all got to come out of camp today and I guess it is the last time out for us. There is some talk around that we will leave next Saturday, the 28th. All of this stuff that I write home to you, please be careful who you tell it to. The wrong person might get hold of it and we might not arrive at our next stop safely.

Well, I don't know much more about what or where we are going. Our company commander said we would be doing a lot of work in our O.D. uniform when we get overseas. That sounds like M.P. duty or Army of Occupation.

I have been issued a lot of new clothes: 1 pair of combat shoes, they are like the paratroopers wear, and 1 pair of regular army shoes, 5 pair of cushion sole sox, 4 hankies, new fatigues, new raincoat, new field jacket, steel helmet, pack, shelter half, mess kit, canteen, cartridge belt, gloves and overseas cap. I had to mark all of it last night with my last initial and last four numbers of my serial number (H-7971).

I got the papers okay and enjoyed reading them. I also got the box that John and Inez sent me. It sure was swell. She had everything imaginable in it.

Mom, as far as my birthday is concerned you don't have to send me anything. I don't have room for anything and we are only allowed so much baggage when we leave. So don't let it worry you. Some day if you are in the buying mood try and find me a good trench knife and holster. I could use one of them but if you can't find a good one it will be okay.

Pop, I haven't forgotten your birthday. The best I could do was send 4 packs of Chesterfields to you. I put them in a box that I sent to Kay so don't forget to get them. I know that a birthday card didn't have to be sent to you so I'll just wish you a Happy Birthday here and hope that I am back home on our next birthdays.

Well I've got to close now and I guess I'll go back to camp. Write when you can.

LOVE, HARRY JR.

November 16, 1944

Dear Mom and Dad:

Hi Folks, how are you? I am okay and doing fine. We made our trip okay and had a lot of fun but it did get a little tiresome towards the end. I can't tell you where I am yet for safety reasons. Maybe in a couple days I might be able to let you know. I just wrote to Kay for the first time since Sunday and I suppose she is pretty anxious to hear from me like you are. I can't write too much because all of our letters are censored now and I don't want to get in wrong with the censor right from the start.

I don't know what my new address is yet but you should be getting a post card with my own new address on it pretty soon. If you don't get one for a while just send your letters to my old address and they will be forwarded on to me here.

Pop, you asked me in your last letter what I wanted you to do with the stock at the garage, the only thing I could figure out to do is to **b**uy **o**ur **s**tock **t**o **o**ffset **N**ovember's sales.* Write and let me know what you make out of it.

Well folks write when you can and I'll do the same.

LOVE, HARRY JR.

---

* Censors would not allow location to be revealed so an acrostic was used to spell out BOSTON.

Friday, November 17, 1944
Somewhere in the East

Dear Mom and Dad:

How are you? Okay I hope. I am fine but I have a slight cold but it is probably from the change of the climate. Ever since we got here it has been cold and raining. This afternoon we were outside all afternoon and it was raining and the rain froze on our steel helmets.

We had our first mail call this evening and I got 2 letters from Kay and also your letter, Mom, that you wrote on Sunday afternoon.

Pop, you had better think again about me going across. I've practically got one foot on the ship and one on the ground. I don't know when we will leave; it may be 2 days or 2 weeks. That is something no one will know and when.

[CENSORED]

Yes, I read about Joe Martin's death. It's too bad, but it is good that he died as easy as he did. I wonder what Frances and her mother will do now. Frances will have to settle down and get herself a good steady job.

I'll bet that football game was a dandy Friday night. I suppose the high school has only a couple more games to play.

Yes, I remember Dice Echelberger but I don't believe I know that Leon Mason that she married. I haven't received the papers as yet. They of course went to Camp McCoy and then had to be forwarded on to me here.

I suppose you got my change of address card okay. I talked to Kay on the phone last night and she had gotten hers okay. I'm sorry I had to ask you for some money but honestly I am flat broke and this is a bad time to be broke. I have to get a haircut and buy writing material and will also want to buy candy and cigarettes on board ship. Last Sunday I had 86 cents and I went to a show which was 15 cents and then on the way coming east I tried to make the remaining 70 cents into $70.00 and of course lost but I finally did manage to win 16 packs of cigarettes which will last me quite a while. Kay also told me you subscribed for the *Gazette* for me. That is sure swell. I will get them okay overseas but if you sent them once a week, I doubt if they would accept the big package.

Well, I've got to close now. I'll probably get to write once or twice more before we leave here. Please don't worry about me. I told Kay I was going to cheat her out of the $10,000 and come back in one piece. I'm not worried about it at all so I can't see why you should worry too much. Just live from one day to the next like I will be doing and then after I walk down Main Street in Berlin maybe I'll stop over at home before I go to Tokyo. It won't take too long so just keep waiting and writing and don't forget the writing.

ALL OF MY LOVE TO YOU BOTH,
HARRY JR.

Sunday 5 P.M.
November 19, 1944

Dear Mom & Dad:

Well I'm still hanging around here in the U.S.A. but for how long I cannot say. I got a letter from Pop yesterday and I got your letter Mom this noon. Things are still the same here. It finally cleared up and the sun was out all day.

That is tough that you had trouble with the car last Sunday night but I suppose it had to happen sometime. So far I haven't got the money or papers from you. I'm going to check up on the money tomorrow and see if it is here and I haven't received notice of it yet.

I suppose it is hard to find a good knife for me. It has to be good because it will be used for more than sharpening pencils. I hope not but I'm not going to be without one when the time comes to use it. I've had a lot of practice on how to use one since I left home and also the use of Jiu Jitsu so you can see I'm trying to be good in all the angles let alone shooting. I honestly am not worried about going into combat. I have a lot of confidence in myself, but not too much, and I am ready to match my skills and tricks against any of them.

Mom, please don't worry about my health. I am perfectly okay I had a slight cold when we first got here but it is gone now. [CENSORED] any kind of weather. Laying on the cold ground and in the rain is practically the same as being at home to me any more. [CENSORED]

I wrote a card to Grandmother Eckstein the other day but honestly I don't know what to have her or even you folks send me for Christmas or any other time. When I get over I will need a lot of foot powder and razor blades and some Band-Aids will probably come in handy too along with food to eat. But you send what you want to and I'll guarantee that it will come to some good use. We can find a use for anything at anytime even if we have to carry it with us until the time comes to use it.

I didn't know that that guy lost that money. I don't doubt but what he flashed it around and told everyone he had it. He better learn to keep his mouth shut before it is too late.

Well, I'm going to close now and sit around and read and shoot the bull a while. Oh yes, I fixed it up this A.M. so Kay will get my overseas bonus by a separate check each month. I won't need it and I'd sooner let her and Martha Kay have it any way. My ten-thousand-dollar insurance policy is okay so I'm all set.

Write when you can. You both write letters that give me a lot of encouragement even if you don't realize it. I'll be careful and keep my head and rear end down too, Pop.

All my love,
Harry Jr.

Tuesday 2:30 P.M.

Dear Mom and Dad:

Just a short line to let you know that I received the money today, in fact not more than 10 minutes ago. Thanks a million for it. You didn't have to double it but I'll not argue with you about it. I'll be careful with it and use it wisely.

It is pouring down rain up here now and it is almost sleet. We were out in it a while this morning but we are staying inside this afternoon. Everything is going along as well as can be expected. We are just laying around waiting. I went to a dance at the #1 Service Club last night. It was too crowded to dance even half way decent. The women up here are built like barrels and sure couldn't take any beauty prizes.

Well I'll close now and write again tomorrow or Thursday. Thanks again for the $20.00. I'll get twenty dollars worth of [CENSORED] hide as quick as I can.

LOVE, HARRY JR.

Wednesday 11/22/44

Dear Pop:

Just have time to write a few lines. I want to let you know that I subscribed to the *Yank* magazine today for 52 weeks and it will come up to your house. I know you will like it. It has a lot of inside stories about the war and also a lot of pictures. A civilian can't buy it at all but I can, and have it sent to you. I hope you enjoy it. I suppose it will start in 2 or 3 weeks.

I am still okay and everything is still running okay up here but will be coming to a head shortly. We are having some snow today and it is fairly cold.

I got the money order cashed okay last night and then I bought some writing paper and envelopes and that is all. I wrote and told Kay this A.M. that whoever sends me a Christmas box could send me some heavy wool sox, size 11 and olive drab color, if you can get it, or white. If each one would send a pair or 2 it wouldn't put all that weight on just one person. I also told her to send some handkerchiefs but don't buy any, I have plenty of old ones at home that will work okay.

I've got to close now. Hope to hear from you both soon.

LOVE, HARRY JR.

Overseas

Somewhere on the Atlantic

Dear Mom and Dad:

Well here I am sailing the ocean blue. The first day out I was okay and then the second day I got sick and now I am okay. It is awful rough out here and everybody has been or still is sick. They have great big cans all over the ship and you can always see 2 or 3 fellows sticking their heads in one of them losing their breakfast or supper. We eat 2 meals a day on here, breakfast and supper, and then we have a snack for dinner. In the mess hall the tables are high and we have to stand up to eat.

You folks were probably eating your turkey dinner

[CENSORED].

The Red Cross gave us coffee and donuts at the pier and of course the band was playing too. Yesterday the Red Cross gave us each a little bag and in it was these things: 1 pack of cigarettes, writing paper, envelopes, pencil, razor blades, soap dish, a small cake of Swan soap, candy, shoe laces and a pocket size story book. We wear our life jackets everywhere we go. We joined another convoy some time last night and it sure is a sight to see so many ships plowing through this rough sea.

Well I've got to close now, it is awful hard to write with this ship rocking like it is. But I just wanted you to know that I am okay.

I don't know when you'll get this letter or when I'll get mail from you but I hope it isn't too far off. I will send a cable to Kay when I reach the other side. Keep writing and I'll do my best.

LOVE, HARRY JR.

P.S. Mom, don't worry, we've got them on the run and they'll probably be quitting very soon now. I'll be careful and I'll probably have a foggy Christmas.

Somewhere on the Atlantic

Dear Mom and Dad:

Hi folks, how are you? Okay I hope. I am fine and dandy but I think I have lost a little weight so far on this trip but I still feel fine.

We had 3 days of bad weather and the ocean was really rough but it has calmed down quite a lot now and we don't toss around so much. Considering everything, we are having a good trip and a lot of fun. We get all of the candy and cigarettes we need. Cigarettes are 50 cents a carton and we sure have a supply laid up. We also get cigarettes from the Red Cross and a wire and cable company in Marion, Indiana, gave us 2 packs and a cake of soap. I wish I could tell you where we were going but I won't be able to until we get there.

I got 2 *Times Gazettes* the day we came on the ship and I've got them practically memorized by now. They sure will look good over here. All we do is eat, sleep and read and try to stay out of details. It has been too rough for any physical training. Well I'll close and hope to hear from you soon. Write when you can and don't worry.

LOVE, HARRY JR.

WAR & NAVY
DEPARTMENTS
V–MAIL SERVICE

OFFICIAL BUSINESS

U.S. POSTAL SERVICE
DEC 13
4 AM
1944
No. 3

PENALTY FOR PRIVATE USE TO AVOID
PAYMENT OF POSTAGE, $300
(PMGC)

FROM
35637971
Pvt. Harry B. Hamilton Jr.
Co. A, 417ᵗʰ Inf. Reg't. A.P.O. 17831
℅ Postmaster New York, N.Y.

TO
Mr. & Mrs. Harry B. Hamilton
205 W. Liberty St
Ashland, Ohio
U.S.A.

(Sender's complete address above)

SEE INSTRUCTION NO. 2

PASSED BY
U.S. ARMY
BASE
CENSOR
(CENSOR'S STAMP)

Somewhere on the Atlantic.

Dear Mom & Dad:

Hi, folks, how are you? O.K. I hope. I am fine & dandy but I think I have lost a little weight so far on this trip but I still feel fine.

We had 3 days of bad weather & the ocean was really rough but it has calmed down quite a lot now and we don't toss around so much. Considering every thing, we are having a good trip & a lot of fun. We get all of the candy & cigarettes we need. Cigarettes are 50¢ a carton and we sure have a supply laid up. We also got cigarettes from the Red Cross & a wire & cable company in Marion, Indiana gave us 2 packs and a cake of soap. I wish I could tell you where we were going but I won't be able to until we get there.

I got 2 Times Gazettes the day we came on the ship & I've got them practically memorized by now. They sure will look good over here. All we do is eat, sleep & read & try to stay out of details. It has been to rough for any physical training. Well I'll close & hope to hear from you soon. Write when you can & don't worry. Love

Harry Jr.

HAVE YOU FILLED IN COMPLETE ADDRESS AT TOP?

PREPAID BY
V–MAIL

HAVE YOU FILLED IN COMPLETE ADDRESS AT TOP?

Somewhere??

Dear Mom and Dad:

Hi folks, how are you? Okay I hope. I just finished writing to Kay and I've got plenty of time so I thought I'd better write a few lines to you.

Well, I am here and I am okay. It will be a couple days before we get straightened around over here and we aren't allowed to tell where we are or anything yet. But we are all okay and we are eating every day and are also in out of the weather. I have seen lots of things that I would like to tell you about but I'll have to wait for a while.

It is hard to realize that I am so far away from home but I wouldn't trade this trip for anything. It is a great thrill and experience and if a lot of the people back in the States would get to see what I have they might wake up and realize there is a war going on. I'm sure glad though that you don't have to put up with the things these people over here have to.

I'll write more when I can and I will probably be getting mail from you all in a few days I hope. If you happen to see Bill Dick tell him I said "Hello" and I'll answer his letter as soon as I can. But I suppose he is way down south for the winter by this time. Write when you can and don't worry about me. I am okay.

LOVE, HARRY JR.

Thursday Night
12/7/44

Dear Mom and Dad:

This is the second letter in 2 days to you folks but I am able to tell you a lot more in this one that I could in the other one. I just got done writing a 9 page letter to Kay and you ask her about what was in it because I probably won't have time to tell you as much as I did her. It is 10 o'clock over here now and that makes it 4 o'clock in the afternoon over home.

I am in south England and we are living in a town in large homes that have been evacuated by the people who have moved to the country and have turned their homes over to the government for the duration. We finally got the place cleaned up and into a fairly decent living quarters. Five of us fellows are in one room and we sure have it fixed nice. We have a fireplace and 3 double deck beds and a table and 2 long benches and a nice big mirror. We keep the floor clean by sweeping and mopping everyday and it is pretty good for us. This house we are in was awful filthy the night we got here but we were so tired we flopped on the floor and what beds there were. There are about 15 to 18 rooms in this house and I think almost every one has a fireplace in it.

Of course at night everything is completely blacked out except for the gas streetlights and they don't throw off very much light. Everybody over here rides a bicycle and there are very few automobiles around. I did see a Ford today with a 19-inch tire rim on it. They have some nice double deck buses that run in the daytime. We go on hikes everyday and it is just like a sight seeing tour. We walk all around town and look the homes over. All the houses here are built out of stone and brick and every house has a high fence or shrubbery around it.

We got our money changed over to English money today and it is going to be hard to get used to using it. We haven't had any passes yet but we are all anxious to get down town and look it over.

Pop, do you think you can get a hold of some more sardines and cheese and crackers or some smoked summer sausage or something that would stand the trip over here? If you can please do and send them to me. Take this letter to the post office and when they see that I requested it they will let you send me a box up to 5 lbs. I think. Send anything that will not spoil and I'll sure be glad to get it.

I've got to close now. I am okay and I am seeing and learning a lot of things. Don't worry about me but don't forget to write. We get mail in a couple days.

LOVE, HARRY JR.

Wednesday, December 13, 1944

Dear Mom and Dad:

Well I feel pretty good tonight. I finally got some mail today and it all came from you folks. I got your letters Mom, that you wrote on Sunday, November 19th, and Wednesday, November 22, and Pop's letter of the 22nd too. So far I haven't heard from Kay but I will in a day or two now. Before I forget it there is one thing I want you to send me and that is 6-cent airmail stamps. We can't get a hold of any over here and my letters will get home a lot quicker by airmail. You can enclose a few in your letters every once in a while.

I know all about that telephone strike you had back home. Some of the fellows couldn't call home on account of it. It delayed my call to Kay about an hour and a half. I hope they wake up back home soon. If they could see what I see they sure would change their minds, such as the bombed out districts, the hundreds of airplanes we see flying around going to or coming from their targets and how the English people have to do without so many things. Little kids running around without hardly any clothes on. Some of our fellows were in London on Monday and Tuesday and they had 3 air raids while they were there. I guess those robot bombs really tear the hell out of things. I am going to London next week for a couple of days.

Well we are getting along okay so far. We sure are walking a lot of miles every day and my poor feet sure do ache sometimes.

I got one of those bulletins that your Sunday School class is sending out while I was back in "Camp Secret." That is a lot better than writing the letters.

I hope you got the letter about the money. I got it okay and still have some of it. Don't worry I am going to have fun. If I wouldn't I'd go nuts sitting around. We have a big Red Cross club and also a Service Club and a few beer joints. So I guess we will get along okay. We are going to be able to buy American beer at the P.X. starting Monday. We are rationed to 7 packs of cigarettes a week, 4 bars of candy.

Pop, I'm glad you got to see the manager of that store about the parts for the garage. He was right in what he said.

You can write to me anything you want to. Your letters won't be censored so ask all the questions you want to and I'll try and answer them if I can.

Well I am getting sleepy and I guess I'm running out of words too so I guess I'll close. Don't worry about me and *keep writing*. If anything new happens I'll try and let you know if I can. You can send me money if you want to Pop, but don't think that it is compulsory. I'll appreciate it all.

LOVE, HARRY, JR.

The snow in this photo taken Christmas, 1944 in Mansfield, Ohio, looks almost as deep as it was in Belgium when I received this photo from Kay.

Dec. 16, 1944

Dear Mom and Dad:

I received your letters of November 20 and 23 and I answered them by regular letter Thursday night. So far I haven't heard from Kay but I am patiently waiting.

I was on K.P. today and got done about 6:30 tonight. We are going to have chicken tomorrow for Sunday dinner. Mom, you should hear all the church bells and chimes over here on Sunday morning. They sure are pretty.

I got my Private First Class rating Thursday. It means $4.80 a month more for me. I was sort of surprised to get it but hope to add more to it as time goes on.

Pop, in your letter to me you said that **B**ill **O**verly **u**sed **r**egular **n**eon **e**lectric **m**arkings **o**n **U**niversals **t**wo **h**ighlights.* I'll bet that made a neat job. I hope it was satisfactory with them.

Well, I've got to close I guess. Tell everyone I said "Hello." Hope you had a Merry Christmas and not too big a hangover New Years Day. Write when you can. I like to hear what goes on at the shop.

LOVE, HARRY JR.

---

* Censor would not allow location to be revealed so an acrostic was used to spell out BOURNEMOUTH.

WAR & NAVY
DEPARTMENTS
V--MAIL SERVICE
OFFICIAL BUSINESS

PENALTY FOR PRIVATE USE TO AVOID
PAYMENT OF POSTAGE, $300

DEC 27
2 AM
1944
No. 3

Print the complete address in plain block letters in the panel above; and your return address in the space provided. Use typewriter, dark ink, or pencil. Write plainly. Very small writing is not suitable.

From
Pvt. Harry B. Hamilton Jr.
35537971
Co B, 417th Inf. BRO 17831
% Postmaster New York N.Y.

To
MR. & MRS. HARRY B. Hamilton
205 W. Liberty St.
Ashland, Ohio.
U.S.A.

PASSED BY
46343
U.S.

DEC. 16 1944
(Date)

Dear Mom & Dad;
I recieved your letters of Nov. 20 & 23 and I answered them by regular letter Thursday night. So far I haven't heard from Kay but I am patiently waiting.
I was on K.P. today and got done about 6:30 tonight. We are going to have chicken tomorrow for Sunday dinner. Mom, you should hear all the church bells and chimes over here on Sunday morning. They sure are pretty.
I got my Private First Class rating Thursday. It means $4.80 a month more for me. I was sort of surprised to get it but hope to add more to it as time goes on.
Pop, In your letter to me you said that Bill Overly used regular neon electric markings on Universals. Two highlights. I'll bet that made a neat job. I hope it was satisfactory with them.
Well, I've got to close I guess. Tell every one I said "Hello". Hope you had a Merry Xmas and not to big a hang over New Years day. Write when you can. I like to hear whats goes on at the shop.
Love
Harry Jr.

V--MAIL

Sunday, January 14, 1945
Somewhere in France

Dear Mom and Dad:

Hi folks, hope you are fine. I am okay and sure am doing some traveling around. We are in France now and the snow is knee deep and it is cold as hell. I got 2 letters from Kay today and also your letter Pop, of the 1st of December, and yours Mom, of the 3rd.

So far I haven't found a knife but in a few days I will be able to find one I think. This sure is a rugged life. If I could tell you how we are living you would hardly be able to believe it. But we are still very much alive and raring to go. George Washington at Valley Forge didn't have anything on us.

I have received a few of the papers and they are a welcome sight. I heard from Kay and she is working. I'm glad she is, it will help her a lot and help pass the time away. It is better for her over there and I told her what I wanted done and I know she won't let me down.

That is too bad that Grandma isn't feeling good. I hope she will get better soon. I don't imagine there is much that can be done for her though.

We have had a few drinks of cognac. It tastes just like moonshine and sure has a kick, but it sure warms you up.

Well I can't think of any more to write now. At least I let you know where I am. Don't worry about me because I'll be okay. We have a good scrappy outfit and I think we'll do okay. The news is good and we'll probably end up in Berlin soon. Just keep writing and that means more to me than a hot meal. I'll write as much as I can and as often as I can. Tell John and Inez and Dale and Sim and everyone I said Hello. Again, don't worry. I'll be okay.

ALL MY LOVE,
HARRY JR.

Wednesday Afternoon
January 17, 1945
Somewhere in France

Dear Mom and Dad:

I wrote you a letter Sunday afternoon but it was a hurry up job so now I will try and write a longer and better one now. I was on guard duty from noon yesterday until noon today and I have this afternoon off and so I have a little time to write. This guard duty is more like the real stuff and we don't have paper wads in our rifles either.

The snow is still here but it is quite a bit warmer now. We are living as good as we can I guess. After we moved the cows out the place started to look like something. We are keeping warm anyway. We have sleeping bags now and they sure are warm. We sleep on straw and have a nice wood fire, which we sit around at night and shoot the bull. Last night we fried bacon in our mess gears and boiled peas and potatoes in the tin cans. We sit around and talk about home and sing and talk about home some more. This may be a rough life but it is what we have all been after ever since we were drafted. We are sure taking a lot more than I think any of us thought we could.

Pop, you asked me about what I thought of our outfit. Well as far as the company is concerned, I know we have the best in the regiment and I know we have the best C.O. in the whole damn Army. He is Captain Robert Bertsch from Akron, Ohio, and he sure is swell. I don't think that there is any man who doesn't like him. He sure looks after us. We have a good platoon leader too, 2nd Lieutenant Jack E. Theall from the south. A lot of the fellows don't think very much of him but if they would stay on the ball he wouldn't have to eat their ass so much. I get along okay with him and I think he is okay. As far as sergeants are concerned we have the best again. All in all this is a swell platoon to be in. It is the only platoon that raises hell and goes out and gets drunk and we all have a lot of fun. It sure is going to be a scrappy outfit and I think we are going places.

Did you receive the *Yank Magazine* yet? I hope so. I sent the money in for it the day we left the States.

We all are having one hell of a time trying to speak French and use French money. Almost all of us are broke now. We had one last big fling before we came to France and all we need money for is our 5 packs of cigarettes and 3 candy bars a week. We are getting a big pay the last of this month and all I owe is 30 francs (60 cents) to our Lieutenant for some airmail stamps. I'll pay him and probably buy cider and cognac and cigarettes with the rest. One French franc is worth 2 cents in our money so I'll sure have a pile of paper when we get paid.

Well I've got to close now and get ready for chow. Mom, don't worry about me. I'm glad you're "traveling" with me but I hope you don't get as tired as we do sometimes. I am okay as far as health and anything else is concerned. I'll write as soon as I can again. So you write also.

ALL MY LOVE,
HARRY JR.

January 25, '45
Somewhere in Belgium

Dear Mom and Dad:

Hi folks, how are you? I am okay. I am in Belgium now. We have done a lot of traveling the past week or so. There is a lot of snow and it is plenty cold too. I got a letter from Mom last night that you wrote December 27th. I also got 6 or 8 letters from Kay and it all was a welcome sight.

I haven't received any of your boxes yet except the one from Mom Wentz. I got about 6 newspapers the other day so I guess they are starting to come through now.

We live in barns, out in the snow or in a room in a Frenchman or Belgian's home and then we sleep on the floor and it is just like heaven to us.

The news sure is good over here and it won't be long and I'll get to see Berlin. I have seen a lot of the damages of war and it sure makes one feel glad that we have to fight over here instead of back in the States. I'll be able to tell you a lot of things some day.

This picture is one I had taken in London. It isn't so hot but you can tell I'm very much alive and if you look close you can see scotch and soda sticking out of my eyes.

I got the paper and the envelope that you enclosed Mom. Don't address them anymore if you send some more because I can't have any identification of my outfit on them at all. I put my return address on the envelopes just before I mail the letters.

Pop how are the fellows at the garage? Tell them I said hello. I didn't stay in France long enough to find any of Dale's girl friends but there are plenty there.

Well I've got to close now I guess. I am okay and haven't been sick at all thank God. I will take care of myself and the Germans too. Right now I am carrying a sub machine gun with me plus my rifle and it sure is a sweet gun.

Well take care of yourselves and you tell everyone I said hello. Please send me another box of food when you can. I'll write every chance I get. Don't worry, I can take it and things could be a lot worse than they are.

LOVE, HARRY JR.

Sunday A.M.
January 29, 1945

Dear Mom and Dad:

Hi folks, hope you are all okay. I am okay even though I am having a little trouble keeping warm. We are up in Luxembourg now and it sure is the nuts. I already have some souvenirs to send home when I get a chance to get a box and mail them. I got 6 letters from Kay and one from each of you last night. Mom's letter was of November 27th and it was mailed with a 3-cent stamp that is why it took so long getting here. Pop's was of January 7 and it was sent airmail. That was a nice little note from Martha Kay and it brought a few tears out.

I won't have a chance to write to John and Inez right away but please tell Inez thanks for such fast service on those cookies. I haven't gotten them yet but I can practically taste them now.

My next raise I hope will be $10.00 a month. If I can earn the Combat Infantryman's Badge I will get that extra 10 a month and it is just as good in my pocket as anyone else's.

I'm doing okay here. We've got a lot of snow and cold weather and of course a lot of noise but you get used to it like you do anything else. We are living pretty good and my buddy Ed Kampshoff (Buffalo) and I have a fairly good time. At least we can keep fairly warm. By the way, this paper I am writing on is German paper.

Well I guess I'll have to close now. I've got to clean my rifle and my sub-machine gun too. Keep writing and don't worry. *I'll come through, I've got to.*

ALL MY LOVE,
HARRY JR.

This photo was taken in London, England, December, 1944 at an American Red Cross service club.

Thursday A.M.
February 1, 1945

Dear Mom and Dad:

Received a letter from each of you last night. Yours, Mom, of the 18 of January, and Pop's of the 14th of January. I sure was glad to get the air mail stamps too because I had just used the last one that Kay had sent me. I hope you both are okay. I am fine myself considering everything. This letter won't be so neat but it is the best I can do under the circumstances. I've got a lot that I would like to tell you but I can't so will have to wait. I am still writing on this German paper and I don't like it but it is all I have until I get to my duffel bag again.

Don't worry Mom, I am behaving okay and I'm taking care of myself. The worst I have had is a runny nose and anyone can have that in this cold weather. It is thawing some here now and it is miserable compared to the cold weather.

That was sure tough about Paul Sattler. He is the first one from the church isn't he? Oh yes, Mom, I got a Christmas card from Lieutenant Mary Schultz and one from Mary K. Weiner and one from Grace Harry. Will you please thank them for me. Have Helen write to Mary and thank her for me. I'm not going to buy anything to send home. What I've got now didn't cost a cent and I hope to send them to Kay soon, so Pop you can get them and take it to the garage and show the rest of the guys. It took 17 days for your letter to get here and 13 for Mom's, which isn't bad at all. I haven't received any boxes yet but I am patiently waiting.

Write when you can and I'm doing my best. I'm doing as you say Pop and making every one count. You know, one for me and one for you and on down the line. Don't worry.

LOVE, HARRY JR.

February 6, 1945
Somewhere in Luxembourg

Dear Mom and Dad:

Hi folks. I'm still okay and the weather here is much warmer. I got the box of sox and hankies and thanks a lot they sure are swell and I needed them too. I got Pop's letters of December 10, 17 and 24, and Mom, yours of January 11 and another one I forgot the date, also Pop's of January 20.

I'm glad to hear that you got the *Yank Magazine* okay. You'll probably be reading about me in it pretty soon. You get a lot of war news in there that doesn't even reach the newspapers.

You sure must have had a lot of snow back there. I'll bet Martha Kay had a big time on the sled. I just finished writing a V-Mail to her and a letter to Kay.

I haven't seen Drushel or Jenkins for a long time. I saw Raymond Clark in France one day but that is all.

Well, this old war is still going on but I don't think it will last too long now. At least we all hope so. When I come home and tell you all that I have seen and done you sure will be surprised. But I'm glad we are fighting this over here instead of back home. This is a terrible mess. I wish I could say more about it but it will have to wait.

I haven't received any of the other boxes yet. I'm anxious to get them all especially John and Inez's because I sure am dry. I suppose I'll get them all in one day. But I'll sure take care of the food and enjoy myself.

I've got to close now and I'll write again as soon as I can. I'll wire you collect when I get in the middle of Berlin but I think the Russians are going to beat me to it.

I'm being careful and I'll be home as soon as I finish my job with these Krauts. Don't worry and take it easy.

LOVE, HARRY JR.

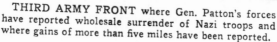

THIRD ARMY FRONT where Gen. Patton's forces have reported wholesale surrender of Nazi troops and where gains of more than five miles have been reported.

Someone clipped and saved this article and map from *The Cleveland Press* for me. It was probably during or around the action mentioned here that Captain Bertsch was killed. Another newspaper article stated "Captain Bertsch and his doughboys stood firm against three counter-attacks and knocked out tanks with bazooka guns. Captain Bertsch was posthumously awarded the Distinguished Service Cross for heroism."

New Blows Struck By Third Army

By LARRY NEWMAN

WITH THE U. S. THIRD ARMY, Germany, Feb. 13—The U. S. Third army struck a series of powerful new blows against the defenses of the western Reich today as the Fourth and 88th infantry divisions linked up their bridgeheads across the Sure and Our rivers for a distance of ten miles.

These combined forces surged forward against the Nazi lines until their hold had been deepened to two miles.

Simultaneously the veteran 76th division whipped into Echternach-Erbuck across the river from the city of Echternach, and drove the Nazis from the town.

Other columns of Lieut. Gen. George S. Patton's command smashed into the frontier town of Vianden and drove the Germans from their last foothold in Luxembourg.

With the proud little Duchy cleared of the enemy, the hard-hitting Fourth infantry finished the job of cleaning troublesome snipers out of the German communications hub of Pruem.

To the northeast of Pruem the Germans assembled their forces and launched two powerful counter-attacks but both were driven off by the Fourth infantrymen with heavy losses to the Nazis.

This article tells of how the Third Army that I was in advanced deeper into Nazi lines.

In Hospital

Wednesday Feb 14, 1945

Dear Mom and Dad:

Well, finally the wicked gets to rest. I am in a hospital back in the rear area. I have trench foot. It is nothing to worry about. My feet got wet and cold and I couldn't massage them or change sox and they swelled up and now I can't walk. I will have to stay in bed here for a while I guess.

This sure is a welcome rest to me. I get plenty to eat and candy, gum and cigarettes of course. The hard part about it is getting used to the bedpan but I'll master that in time. There absolutely is no need to worry about me. I will be fixed up in good shape. They have been putting ice packs on my feet to draw the temperature out of them. They sure did hurt and burn and ache Monday afternoon and the medic looked at my feet and picked me up and carried me to a jeep and brought about 8 or 10 of us back here.

Well Pop, I suppose you will be reading about us or maybe you already have in your newspaper or the *Yank*. I told you we had a scrappy outfit and we sure proved it.

Well, I've got to close now. I'll write as often as I can while I'm here resting. Don't worry, I'll be okay. We can thank God that it is just my feet. You keep writing to the same address. I won't get any of your mail here but I'll sure have a lot to read when I get back to my company. Tell everyone I said "Hello" and *Don't Worry.*

LOVE, HARRY JR.

Print the complete address in plain letters in the panel below, and your return address in the space provided on the right. Use typewriter, dark ink, or dark pencil. Paint or small writing is not suitable for photographing.

PASSED BY
U 618 S
ARMY EXAMINER

TO: Mr. & Mrs. Harry B. Hamilton
205 W. Liberty St.
Ashland, Ohio.
U. S. A.

FROM
Cpl. H. Hamilton Jr. 35837971
Co. A. 417th Inf. A.P.O. 76
c. Postmaster New York, N. Y.

SEE INSTRUCTION NO. 2

(Sender's complete address above)

Dear Mom & Dad: Friday, Feb. 16, 1945

Just in case you haven't received my letter that I
wrote to you on the 13th yet I will tell you again that I
am in a hospital in France. I have a case of trench foot.
I am getting along O. K. but I have to stay in bed and
that is hard to do. But my feet are swollen & sore so I
will have to stay off of them. We are sure getting plenty
to eat and of course will get caught up on our sleep.
I won't get any mail while I am here so I will have a
lot to read when I get back to my company. I don't
know how long it will be before I get back but I imagine
it will be sometime after the first of March. There is no
need to worry about me because I am O. K. and I have
nothing wrong with me that rest won't cure. I'll take
care of myself & do as they tell me too do. You keep on writing
to my same address & if there are any changes made I'll
let you know right away. Maybe I'll have a chance to
catch up on my letter writing while I am here.

Well, let's hope the news keeps on being good so the
end will come soon. I'll write and let you know as much
as I can. Please don't worry. I'm O. K.
                                                          love
                                                          Harry Jr.

HAVE YOU FILLED IN COMPLETE
ADDRESS AT TOP?

REPLY BY
V----MAIL

HAVE YOU FILLED IN COMPLETE
ADDRESS AT TOP?

Friday, February 16, 1945

Dear Mom and Dad:

Just in case you haven't received my letter that I wrote to you on the 14th yet I will tell you again that I am in a hospital in France. I have a case of trench foot. I am getting along okay, but I have to stay in bed and that is hard to do. But my feet are swollen and sore so I will have to stay off of them. We are sure getting plenty to eat and of course will get caught up on our sleep. I won't get any mail while I am here so I will have a lot to read when I get back to my company. I don't know how long it will be before I get back but I imagine it will be sometime after the first of March. There is no need to worry about me because I am okay and I have nothing wrong with me that rest won't cure. I'll take care of myself and do as they tell me to do. You keep on writing to my same address and if there are any changes made I'll let you know right away. Maybe I'll have a chance to catch up on my letter writing while I am here.

Well, let's hope the news keeps on being good so the end will come soon. I'll write and let you know as much as I can. Please don't worry, I'm okay.

LOVE, HARRY JR.

Print the complete address in plain letters in the panel below, and your return address in the space provided on the right. Use typewriter, dark ink, or dark pencil. Faint or small writing is not suitable for photographing.

PASSED BY
018 61 S
ARMY EXAMINER

TO:
Mr. & Mrs. H.B. Hamilton
205 W. Liberty St.
Ashland, Ohio
U.S.A.

SEE INSTRUCTION NO. 2

FROM
Pfc. H. Hamilton Jr. 35837971
Co. A, 417th Inf. A.P.O. 76
% Postmaster, New York N.Y.
(Sender's complete address above)

Dear Mom & Dad!   Monday Feb. 19, 1945

Hi folks, hope you are all O.K. I am coming along fine. My feet are getting better slow but sure. I had a little trouble with my bowels but they are better now too. They didn't feed me any thing for a while and then started giving me soup & pudding & something light. I guess I will get to eat a regular dinner this noon. The American Red Cross was around yesterday and gave us coffee & donuts. I had to save my donuts until this morning but they sure did taste good. I forgot to tell you that I recieved both of your letters of Dec. 31. Don't you worry Pop, your son is more than taking care of himself. I may be a buck or staff sergeant when I get back to my company. I'll let you know more about it later on. In your letter you said that Capt. Bertsch got it. That is sure tough. I will probably get a lot of the news when I get my mail and the newspapers. Well I'm running out of space so it is time to close I guess. Don't worry about me, I'm coming along O.K. The only thing that is hard to do around here is use the bed pan. Keep writing. Love
Harry Jr.

HAVE YOU FILLED IN COMPLETE
ADDRESS AT TOP?

REPLY BY
V---MAIL

HAVE YOU FILLED IN COMPLETE
ADDRESS AT TOP?

Monday, February 19, 1945

Dear Mom & Dad:

Hi folks, hope you are all okay. I am coming along fine. My feet are getting better slow but sure. I had a little trouble with my bowels but they are better now too. They didn't feed me anything for a while and then started giving me soup and pudding and something light. I guess I will get to eat a regular dinner this noon.

The American Red Cross was around yesterday and gave us coffee and donuts. I had to save my donuts until this morning but they sure did taste good. I forgot to tell you that I received both of your letters of December 31. Don't you worry Pop, your son is more than taking care of himself. I may be a buck or staff sergeant when I get back to my company. I'll let you know more about it later on. In your letter you said that Captain Bertsch got [CENSORED]. That is sure tough. I will probably get a lot of the news when I get my mail and the newspapers. Well I'm running out of space so it is time to close, I guess. Don't worry about me I'm coming along okay. The only thing that is hard to do around here is use the bedpan. Keep writing.

LOVE, HARRY JR.

Print the complete address in plain letters in the panel below, and your return address in the space provided on the right. Use typewriter, dark ink, or dark pencil. Faint or small writing is not suitable for photographing.

TO
Mr. & Mrs. Harry B. Hamilton
205 W. Liberty St.
Ashland, Ohio.
U.S.A.

[CENSOR'S STAMP]   SEE INSTRUCTION NO. 2

FROM
Pfc. H. Hamilton Jr. 35837971
Detachment of Patients
4126 U.S.A. Hosp. Plant, A.P.O. 68
℅ Postmaster New York, N.Y.
(Sender's complete address above)

Dear Mom & Dad: 2/23/45
        I am in a hospital somewhere in
England now. I have a new address, my name
and serial number and then:
        Detachment of Patients
        4126 U.S.A. Hosp. Plant, A.P.O. 68
        ℅ Postmaster New York, N.Y.
They will send all of my mail from my company
back here to me.
        Would you please send me some money?
I haven't been paid for over 2 months & I don't
know when I will get paid. Just put it in an
air mail letter & I'll get it O.K.
        I am O.K. except for my feet and they
ache a lot. I have to stay off of them for
quite a while. Don't worry though because
I will come along O.K. I'll write a letter as
soon as I can find enough to write about.
                        Love,
                        Harry Jr.

HAVE YOU FILLED IN COMPLETE
ADDRESS AT TOP?

REPLY BY
V····MAIL

HAVE YOU FILLED IN COMPLETE
ADDRESS AT TOP?

☆ U. S. GOVERNMENT PRINTING OFFICE : 1943 16—29140-5

2/23/45

Dear Mom and Dad:

I am in a hospital somewhere in England now. I have a new address, my name and serial number and then:

Detachment of Patients
4126 U.S.A. Hosp. Plant, A.P.O. 68
c/o Postmaster New York, N. Y.

They will send all of my mail from my company back here to me.

Would you please send me some money? I haven't been paid for over 2 months and I don't know when I will get paid. Just put it in an airmail letter and I'll get it okay.

I am okay except for my feet and they ache a lot. I have to stay off of them for quite a while. Don't worry though because I will come along okay. I'll write a letter as soon as I can find enough to write about.

LOVE, HARRY JR.

2/25/45

Dear Mom and Dad:

Just a few lines to let you know I am still okay. My feet bother me quite a bit, but I guess it is just going to take time for them to get okay again. This laying in bed and the past has made me pretty nervous but the rest will bring me around I hope. I had my money changed the other day. I had 24 francs (48 cents) and I'm going to buy candy and cookies with it. That is why I asked you for some money because I will need it to buy my rations. I'll probably get your money and then the army will pay me too but I'm not going to take that chance. I will probably be here for quite a while but I'm not sure.

Give Inez my address will you please. I'll write to her and everyone when I feel better and in the mood to write.

I do a lot of reading and we have a radio that helps out too. I get all of Ashland College's basketball scores over the radio. Don't worry about me, I'll be okay. I'll write as often as I can. Take care of yourselves. The news is good and it won't be long now I hope.

LOVE, HARRY JR.

Wednesday 7:00 P.M.
March 7, 1945

Dear Mom and Dad:

I guess I had better write to you although I haven't much to write about. I am just the same and my feet are coming along okay I guess. They are swelled and numb and they ache and it feels like thousands of needles are pricking them. I never thought that they were froze that bad. Maybe you think my feet got this way due to my neglect in taking care of them but it absolutely wasn't. Some day I'll tell you all about it. If I wouldn't have had those sox you sent me I would probably be learning to walk with artificial feet by now.

The American Red Cross just gave us 4 donuts apiece so I'll have something to eat with my eggnog or hot chocolate before lights out tonight. The Red Cross sure is doing some good work over here. When I was in France, Belgium, Luxembourg and Germany they were right there with hot coffee and donuts and cigarettes, candy and gum. They sure are helping a lot of boys out. Just to see an American girl working for them is a good morale builder. We get so tired of seeing these French, Belgium and German civilians and it is hard to talk to them. The French were the easiest for me to talk to. I knew how to ask them for cider and cognac (white lightning) and that was all that was necessary for most of us. What got me was the little kids like Martha Kay. It was freezing weather outside and the poor kids had no stockings on and sometimes not even a coat and never a hat. Their shoes were like cardboard and I don't know how they stayed alive. I used to give them gum and candy and some of my D ration chocolate candy. Their little eyes would just pop out when they saw that and they were your friend for life. A lot of French people work in the hospitals back in France and they are slow workers but they will do anything for you.

I guess I'd better close for now. I haven't received any mail as yet but I will before long. I wrote to John and Inez a day or two ago. Tell everyone I said Hello and that I'm okay. The news is getting better every day. They'll have Hitler hanging by his b____ before long. I hope I get there to see it. Write when you can.

LOVE, HARRY JR.

Saturday 7 P.M.
March 10, 1945

Dear Mom and Dad:

I'm going to start this letter to you tonight but I'm not sure if I'll finish it tonight or tomorrow. I have felt tough all day. My feet ached all day and I was nervous and that upset my stomach and I couldn't eat right. I just finished writing to Kay and it was hard to even write to her.

The Red Cross gave us some more donuts today but I didn't eat any. I told the Red Cross girl that I didn't have a razor and she brought me a swell single edge Gem razor in a black leather case. I've never used a single edge razor but I can get used to it.

We had a good laugh today. A fellow here got a letter from some people back home and it was sent to his company up on the front line, these people didn't know that he was in the hospital. I guess he was fighting at the time the letter was written to him. Anyway these people wanted to know what he did on his weekends. Boy, some people think we fight from 8 in the morning until 4 in the afternoon and have Saturday and Sunday off. It sure did give us a good laugh. You should have heard that fellow blow up when he read that.

Well Mom, this letter is meant especially for you. Your birthday isn't far off and I wanted to make sure that you got this letter before then. If I could walk to the P.X. here at the hospital I'd try to find you a birthday card but that is impossible so far. So I wish you a "Happy Birthday" in this letter. I think this will be a happy birthday for you too. The news is so good and it gets better every day. Maybe Germany will quit around that time. Let's hope so anyhow.

How is the dog coming along? I thought about her today. Since I haven't heard from you for a long time (since February 6) she may be dead by now. You said once she was sick and maybe you had to get rid of her. I can kill Jerries but I couldn't harm her a bit. She's been a good little dog.

I hope you are getting the *Yank Magazine* okay Pop. I get to read it here every week but you save them for me because I want to look over them again and I can maybe tell you more about some of the pictures and articles.

Well I've got to close. My mail should come next week some time. I'm sure looking forward to getting it. Don't worry about me, I'll be okay. I still think that if they would give me a quart I'd get better a lot faster. It's been since I was in London when I had my last good drink. I wish they would bring John and Inez's package in here now. I'd sleep good tonight I'll bet. Keep on writing and I'll write the first of the week again.

LOVE, HARRY JR.

Thursday 6 P.M.
March 15, 1945

Dear Mom and Dad:

There is one soldier in the world that feels good today and that is me. I got 3 letters from Kay, yours Mom of the 6th of March and yours Pop of the 5th plus the welcome $10. Thanks a lot for the money. I got it changed okay. I also got 2 letters from John and Inez and a get well card from Alice Grimm and daughter and the bulletin from the church. Inez wrote that Jr. is living in foxholes and wrote about the Burma Road. I'll bet he has been transferred to the Infantry.

I am still the same as usual. My feet ache but there is positively no danger in losing them. It will just take time for them to get well again. I have to oil them every day so the skin won't crack. I sleep with them out of the covers. If I would cover them up they would burn up. That was plenty of money and I wouldn't have had to write for it if I had been paid but circumstances didn't allow it. Money isn't any good up front anyway. A belt of ammunition does more good then a million dollars would.

No, don't put anything in the paper about me. I don't need any publicity. What I want to get out of this war is me. Publicity is like medals, they don't save your neck. It is okay that you didn't have the paper address changed. It would just be a bother. I may stay here a week, month or 6 months or I may be moved tomorrow. So if I ever move I'll write and tell you to hold up your letters until I send a new address.

Don't worry Pop, I'm a pretty wise fellow now and I keep my eyes and ears open and my mouth shut. A fellow gets smart quick when the lead starts coming at him.

Mom, my eyes still are good because I could read that letter okay without putting anything behind the paper. I sure was glad to hear that Ray Clark got to see his brother. The last I saw Ray was in France. We were waiting on them damn 40 and 8 cars and in snow up to our asses. We only had to wait 9 hours this time. I was in the same attachment that he is.

Mom, you are thinking of me coming home just like Kay is. I sure want to but this war is still on over here and I've got a lot of buddies who will be glad to have me back and helping them, little as it may be. My platoon leader, Lieutenant Theall, told me that he would be waiting for me and he said he would always request for me when he would ask the replacement center for new men. He told me that he had depended on me a lot and that I had never fallen down in doing my duty. He said if there was anything he could do for me while I was back here I should write him. Imagine him up there ducking lead and wanting to help me back here. He even offered me money but I refused it. Of course Kay and Martha Kay and you folks mean more to me than my buddies do and I'll never turn down a chance to come home. I wasn't the only one in bad shape when we came off the line. Some day I'm going to tell you about it, in between my tears. Those boys in my company are real men and I sure was proud to be one of them. They showed what could be done under unusual circumstances and when things got to what we thought was near the end we just got mad as hell and decreased the German population some more.

Pop, I hope you saved those articles in the *Plain Dealer* about Captain Bertsch and the 76th Division. I will want to read them some day. There will never another man as good a leader as he was.

You said that the *Life* magazine of February 12th had the article on trench foot. That was the same day I was taken to the hospital.

I guess I'd better close now. What I've told you about my feet is the truth and they will be okay by 1960 I'm almost sure.

Thanks again for the money. It was plenty. I'll get paid here whenever my records get here from my company.

The news is good and General Patton is on the warpath again. Watch that Third Army go like a streak of sh— when he gives the word. I'm glad we've got a radio here, we get the news hot off the front.

Write when you can and I'll write again in 2 or 3 days. I got Sim's letter yesterday and answered it right away.

LOVE, HARRY JR.

P.S. Surprised to hear from Kay that Shorty Smith and Merle Crandall are in the Army. And the war is going to end quick now because they got Jack Way.

WAR & NAVY
DEPARTMENTS
V–MAIL SERVICE

OFFICIAL BUSINESS

PENALTY FOR PRIVATE USE TO AVOID
PAYMENT OF POSTAGE, $300

To: Mr. & Mrs. H. B. Hamilton
205 W. Liberty St.
Ashland, Ohio.
U.S.A.

From: Pfc. H. Hamilton, Jr. 35537931
Detach. of Patients 4126
U.S.A. Hosp. Plant H.P.o. 68
c/o Postmaster, New York, N.Y.

Friday, March 16, 1945

Dear Mom & Dad:

I just wrote to Kay and told her that I am going to be moved to another hospital so I will have a new address again. So you had better hold up your letters until I send you my new address.

Pop, tell Jim to hold up that box he wanted to send me also. He asked me what he could send me in his letter.

I have felt pretty good today. It has been warm and my feet sting because they are thawing out.

Please tell John & Ivy & everyone else that I will write them and send my new address.

I'll write as soon as I get my new address. I've got to close & eat supper now.

love,

Harry Jr.

HAVE YOU FILLED IN COMPLETE
ADDRESS AT TOP?

V-MAIL

HAVE YOU FILLED IN COMPLETE
ADDRESS AT TOP?

Friday, March 16, 1945

Dear Mom & Dad:

I just wrote to Kay and told her that I am going to be moved to another hospital so I will have a new address again. So you had better hold up your letters until I send you my new address.

Pop, tell Sim to hold up that box he wanted to send me also. He asked me what he could send me in his letter.

I have felt pretty good today. It has been warm and my feet sting because they are thawing out.

Please tell John & Inez & everyone that I will write them and send my new address. I've got to close and eat supper now.

LOVE, HARRY JR.

Yc. H. Hamilton 33 85 19 71
Stark Gen. Hosp.
Charleston S.C.

Dear Mom + Dad:
I am O.K. and am
leaving for Brookes Gen. Hosp.
Fort Sam Houston, near
San Antonio Texas Sunday
morning. I think I'll be
home on a convalescent
leave shortly. This is the
ship I came back over on
& it sure was a dandy.
We had ice cream + milk
every day. My feet are the
same + I sure am hucking
for a discharge. I'll write
when I get to Texas Love
Harry Jr.

POST CARD

NAVY YARD BR.

Mr. & Mrs. H. B. Hamilton
205 W. Liberty St.
Ashland, Ohio.

U. S. HOSPITAL SHIP CHARLES A. STAFFORD
ARRIVES AT PORT OF EMBARKATION
CHARLESTON, S. C.

Photo by U. S. Army Signal Corps

Traveled 450 miles across the ocean on this hospital ship, Charles A. Stafford,
to Charleston, South Carolina.83

Tuesday 4:30 P.M.

Dear Mom and Dad:

Arrived here about 2 hours ago and am okay. Sometime in the next week or so I will be home for a long furlough (45 days) and I'm afraid I'll have to put the touch on you for $20.00. I would appreciate it if you could wire it to me. I think it will be enough and I can pay you back when I collect my ration money after my furlough. I'll get 65 cents a day while I am home.

I'll write more tomorrow if I can get around to it.

LOVE, HARRY JR.

Saturday Eve.

Dear Mom and Dad:

I have copied for you a sort of log on my travels. I kept this in my Testament and I shouldn't have these dates and facts. Please don't show it or mention any of it to anyone except John and Inez. The 76th Division was on the secret list while I was with them and they may still be. If any of this information would get to the paper it would be my neck. I hope you can understand this so-called chart. There is a lot of things that happened that I didn't write but I will be able to tell you them when I see you.

I will leave here this coming Monday or Tuesday and it will take me around 40 hours to come home. Thanks a lot for the money.

I'll see you in a few days so don't write and I won't anymore either.

Believe it or not I am getting whiskey 3 times a day as part of my treatment.

LOVE, HARRY JR.

I carried this photo of Kay and Martha Kay with me and at one point when we were surrounded by Germans, I buried it along with my wedding ring. If we were captured I didn't want to provide any personal information if I could help it.

November 13, 1944, left Camp McCoy, Wisconsin.

November 16, arrived Camp Miles Standish.

November 23, Thanksgiving Day, left Boston on Merchant Marine ship, "The Marine Raven." Loaded on at 1 P.M., left the dock at 2 A.M.

December 4, arrived Plymouth, England. Took train through Essex and South Hampton.

December 5, arrived Bournemouth, England.

January 9, 1945, left Bournemouth, England.

January 10, arrived South Hampton and loaded on English ship.

January 11, arrived LeHavre, France 4 P.M. and hiked 10 miles in foot of snow. Waited in field for trucks until 3 A.M. Take open trailers to Cressy, France. Very cold and snowing.

January 12, arrived Cressy 11 A.M. Cressy is 25 kilo (18 to 20 miles) from Ruen. Moved out the cows and lived in farmer's barn.

January 19, left Cressy 3 A.M. marched to Aussey, France. Stood in snow and cold until 4 P.M. Talked to Raymond Clark for a while. Loaded on 40 [men] and 8 [horses] box cars.

January 20, arrived Reims and stayed in barn about 8 kilo from Reims. Cleaned equipment for action to start in the morning of 21st at 6 A.M. Rode on trucks and tanks, very little action.

January 21, arrived 15 kilo from St. Hubert, Belgium. Got into a lot of woods fighting. Went on first patrol with 12 other men. New man struck match in dark and all hell broke loose.

January 24, pulled back and took trucks on through Bastogne and into Luxemburg.

January 25, arrived 2 kilo from Echternach, on Luxembourg German border at 3 A.M. Relieved 87th Division and took up a defensive position. Lots of snow and very cold here. Took out 8 patrols in 10 days. Patrols were of 6 or 8 men. Very little sleep for 10 days. Most patrols at night going into Echternach and down to Saar River and crossed it once. Had a very close call here with Sargeant Bliss. Two men killed and had to lie in snow 2 1/2 hours before could move out. Given a drink of champagne by Captain Bertsch when we got back to command post.

February 4, relieved by the 5th Division at 7 P.M.. Moved into Echternach at 2 A.M. Lived in cellars of bombed houses.

February 7, attacked across Saar River into Siegfried Line at 1 A.M. using 20 man assault boats (18 infantry and 2 combat engineers). Climbed a very steep and rocky mountain. Blew up pillboxes and saw lots of action. I was in charge of a demolition squad and we had two 35 lb. charges of TNT. Had another close call here. Got stuck in barbed wire and machine gun opened up but made it okay. Was supposed to reach objective at 7 A.M. and arrived there 5 hours late at 12 noon. Dug in 2 1/2 miles inside Siegfried Line in rain, snow and sleet and mud. First battalion of 417th regiment was to hold objective. Out of approximately 600 men only 158 of us made it to objective thanks to Captain Bertsch. We were cut off and surrounded for 4 days and nights. Air Force dropped food, medical supplies and ammunition to us.

February 9, Germans killed our 2 medics. Kennedy killed by sniper but got the sniper before he died. We held off three counter attacks and one tank attack. Captain Bertsch and his runner killed by sniper in afternoon. Two men in a foxhole were given one K ration and one chocolate bar for one day's food supply. Couldn't get out of hole until night. Had to take a crap in a ration box and throw it over the side of hole. Had lots of rain and cold. I went into water almost to my hips when getting out of boat when crossing Saar River and couldn't change clothes or even dry off. All we had to cover up with was our raincoats.

February 12, pulled off line at 3 P.M. Out of the 158 men starting with us only 55 of us came back out of pocket. Medic looked at my feet and picked me up, carried me to an aid station.

February 13, arrived 106th Battallion Hospital at Thionville, France at 2 A.M.

February 14, taken to 92nd Battalion Hospital in Thionville.

February 19, taken to Air Evacuation Hospital at Thionville and flown to Paris February 19th in a C-47 which took 1 hour and 15 minutes.

February 20, left 8th Air Force Evacuation Hospital in Paris and flown 1 hour and 45 minutes to Evacuation Hospital in England, 35 miles from Fruem.

February 22, left Evacuation Hospital and taken to 216th General Hospital near Fruem and Warminister, England.

March 17, taken to 74th General Hospital at Bristol.

March 24, left England, 2 A.M. on Charles A. Stafford Hospital ship.

April 4, Arrived Charleston, South Carolina after 4500 mile trip across the ocean.

Monday A.M.

Dear Mom and Dad:

We arrived in San Antonio about 9:15 last night. About 2 hours out of St. Louis we ran into some high water. Some river was over-flowing and the water was over the tracks and at one place almost over the wheels on the coaches. We had to go slow through this and then we got into a bad storm and that slowed us up too so that is why we were 2 hours late.

So far I haven't done anything except give some urine for analysis. I am in the same annex and ward I was before I came home. So my address is the same as before:

Brooke Gen. & Conv. Hosp.
Ward 62 B Annex 3
Ft. Sam Houston, Texas

It sure is hot and sultry down here but there is a good cool breeze at night. I met a fellow from Parkersburg, West Virginia, in St. Louis. He was down here before with me and we went home together.

In Saturday's St. Louis paper I saw where there is going to be another battle star given besides that Ardennes Forest one. This one will be for Central Europe. I don't know if I will get that one or not but I'm going to see about it.

My feet are burning a lot so I don't know what will happen until I see the doctor, which may not be for 2 or 3 days yet. This hospital is sure crowded. There are a lot of fellows here from Europe.

Well, I'll close for this time. Give John and Inez my address. I'll write again when I learn something new.

LOVE, HARRY JR.

Monday

Dear Mom and Dad:

Well I am finally settled. My new address is Co. H-3, Brooke Convalescent Hospital, Ft. Sam Houston, Texas. Please tell John and Inez and also Sponslers.

This is a lot better here. We can get around and go to town or play ball, golf or ride horses or go swimming. I should be here from 4 to 8 weeks. It just depends on my feet I guess.

Mom, have they got any of those T-shirts at the store? If so will you please get 2 or 3 and send them to me and I'll tell Kay to pay you for them. I'll take a medium or size 36.

I'll write again in a couple days. It is 3:45 and I have to eat at 4 o'clock. Have Kay show you the letters I got from Smitty and Jr.

I was issued a pair of shorts to wear and also I will get another pair of these low shoes.

I was out to the zoo yesterday. It is a big place and there is a lot of animals there. At least it helped pass away the time.

Well I'll close now. Write when you can.

LOVE, HARRY JR.

Friday Eve.

Dear Mom and Dad:

I received your letter, Mom, this noon and so I will answer it now and then when I hear from Pop I will be able to write again. It sure is plenty hot down here. All I wear in the daytime is a pair of shorts and am I ever getting brown. We have an 18-hole golf course here and it sure is a swell one. I played the first 9 Wednesday afternoon and had a 50. I was going to play this morning but they didn't have any balls. If you haven't sent those shirts yet, get into my golf bag and send me 8 or 10 balls.

You asked what I have to do here. I have to answer a roll call at 8 A.M. and 4:30 P.M. the rest of the time I can go golfing, swimming, horseback riding, pitch horseshoe or bicycle riding or almost anything, even go into town. I am getting no treatment of any kind. Before I came home on furlough they told us that smoking wouldn't hurt us and now they have changed their minds again and tell us not to smoke but to drink whiskey when we get a chance. We can have all the whiskey we want right here in the barracks. They say that smoking clogs up the blood vessels in our feet. I don't think they actually do know what to do for our feet. The other morning a doctor took our blood pressure and then we had to put our feet in ice water and he took our pressure again. Of course our pressure went up because your heart beats faster from the shock of the cold water. That ice water made my legs ache clear up to my hips. I only had my feet in there for about 30 seconds but it sure was painful.

I was to the dentist again yesterday morning and had 3 small fillings put in. It didn't bother me a bit. I would like to stay here until August 12th at least. Then I can put in for my 6 months insurance payments. If they don't pay me pretty soon I'll be broke as it is. Some fellows that came back from furlough with me have been paid twice already. The payroll department and record department are run by civilians and they sure don't work, only when the big shot comes around. I will probably have to talk till I am blue to get that Ardennes Star but I'll get it in time. I am not eligible for the Central European Star. That is for around the Rhine River.

I think I know who that soldier was who had that burnt face. That comes from that white phosphorus. It sure can mess a fellow up.

Well I've got to close now. I'll write more later on. If there is anything you want to know just ask me and I'll try and answer it.

LOVE, HARRY JR.

Hi MarthaKay:
Have a good time at Grandmas
& be sure & behave. I'll be home
soon. all my love & kisses
x x x x Daddy.

UNITED STATES ARMY

Monday Eve
July 2, 1945

Dear Mom & Dad:
I recieved your letter of the 28th
this noon. It is 5:15 now & supper is over
so I can write without being disturbed. I
don't know if I told you or not that I am
getting the Times Gazette now. I have recieved
about 6 or 7 so far. Well since my last letter
to you there has been a few changes made here.
Last Friday we were told that at least 80%
of us will get discharged and now we are all
trying to be one of them. I already have one
clearance in my favor. I have to have my
chest X-rayed, my eyes tested & my feet checked
after a 5 mile hike. We will be able to put in
for pension immediatly after discharged. The
most we can get is 62½% disability which
would amount to $62.50 per month but I know
there will be very few that get that much.
We can put in for that and be satisfied
with $25.00 or less. There is more red tape to
go through to get out of this army than there
was to get in. I have to see the doctor again
Wednesday morning, so I am keeping my fingers
crossed.
If that show "Ernie Pyles Story of G.I. Joe comes
to Ashland be sure & see it. It is exactly like I was
in. It shows fighting in towns & life in a fox hole.
It is a real good show.
I've got to close now. I'll write the last of
this week & I hope I can give you some good news.
Love
Harry Jr.

Monday Eve
July 2, 1945

Hi Martha Kay:
Have a good time at Grandma's
and be sure and behave. I'll be home
soon. All my love & kisses
XXXX Daddy.

Dear Mom and Dad:

I received your letter of the 28th this noon. It is 5:15 now
and supper is over so I can write without being disturbed. I don't
know if I told you or not that I am getting the *Times Gazette*
now. I have received about 6 or 7 so far.

Well since my last letter to you there has been a few changes
made here. Last Friday we were told that at least 80% of us will
get discharged and now we are all trying to be one of them. I
already have one clearance in my favor. I have to have my chest
x-rayed, my eyes tested and my feet checked after a 5-mile hike.
We will be able to put in for pension immediately after discharged. The most we can get is 62% disability which would
amount to $62.50 per month but I know there will be very few
that get that much. We can put in for that and be satisfied with
$25.00 or less. There is more red tape to go through to get out of
this army than there was to get in. I have to see the doctor again
Wednesday morning, so I am keeping my fingers crossed.

I can't find that letter of Smitty's. I probably mislaid it, when
I find it I will send it to you. It didn't have any information in it

about the other fellows except that there are only 16 original men left of our platoon. He told me he was having a good time with the women. Because he can talk German, he picks out the best looking ones for himself and lets the other boys take what is left. I wrote and told him to tell me about a lot of the fellows and to let me know anything else he can.

They aren't using that ice water treatment anymore. I guess it was a flop just like everything else they have tried. My legs still hurt up to my knees from it and I have sure let the doctor know about it.

I don't need anything to eat. We get plenty here, more than we can eat sometimes.

I'm still after that battle star and to get paid. I wear myself out trying to go to all those places and talk to those guys.

If that show "Ernie Pyles Story of GI Joe" comes to Ashland be sure and see it. It is exactly like I was in. It shows fighting in towns and life in a foxhole. It is a real good show.

I've got to close now. I'll write the last of this week and I hope I can give you some good news.

LOVE, HARRY JR.

Sunday
July 8th, 1945

Dear Mom and Dad:

It is about time to go eat dinner but I will start this letter
anyway. Everything is about the same here. I had my chest x-
rayed and my blood test taken yesterday morning. It will take
until Wednesday or Thursday for the x-ray to come back and if it
and the blood test is okay I will get my discharge within a week
or 10 days. I also got paid $64.00 yesterday and of course drank
a few beers last night. I took a 5-mile hike Thursday morning
and the doctor cleared my feet and eyes Friday morning. I sure
hope my x-ray and blood test go through okay. I want to get out
and get settled somewhere before Martha Kay starts to school. I
have a good chance to take Harold Sponsler's store over and if I
can get the cash, that is what I will do. I don't want to go back to
work in a shop unless I have to. But it is hard to tell what will
happen.

Yesterday afternoon I was over to Randolph Field. I took 2
airplane rides. The first one was in a B-25, a medium bomber,
and the last one was in a P-4, a navy fighter plane. That last one
was a dandy. We went 240 M.P.H. and it sure was a thrill. I also
got to go inside a B-29. That is the biggest bomber built.

This afternoon I am going out to Brackenridge Park again.
All they have out there is the zoo and beer but I get tired of looking at this camp all week and this is sure a nice place to go and
watch the animals and the women.

I've got to close now and go and eat dinner. I'll write the middle of this week again when I find out more about my discharge.

LOVE, HARRY JR.

I hope Martha Kay was good while she was there with you.

Sunday Afternoon
July 22nd

Hi Folks:

I received your letter, Mom, this noon and I have a lot of time to waste so I decided to answer it right away. I also am sending you a letter that I just got from Smitty this past week. I am moving to Company D-1 in the morning. I don't know if that is good or bad but I think it is good. My new address will be Company D-1, 900 Area, Brooke Convalescent Hospital, Ft. Sam Houston, Texas.

You asked about the blood test and x-ray. I don't know if they were okay or not. The doctor has never called me in to have them taken again or for any further check up so I guess they must be okay. I have lost 3 lbs. since I have been back but I can blame that on the heat I guess.

Mom, if you can get those T-shirts you go ahead and get them and don't send them unless I write and tell you to again. If I don't get discharged I will be home on furlough pretty soon so either way I can get them when I get home.

I didn't hear about Leland Smith getting hurt. I don't think it was in the paper, if it was I missed it. I saw where Howard Drushel's brother-in-law, Paul Gertgey, was killed on April 26th in Europe. That sure is hard on the Drushel family.

Well there is nothing new here so I can't tell you anything more. I'll write again after I find out what this Company D-1 deal is about.

LOVE, HARRY JR.

My father was honorably discharged from the U.S. Army on July 27, 1945. Within two weeks he was back to work at Mansfield Tire and Rubber in Mansfield Ohio and shortly thereafter, he and my mother bought a house in Mansfield. Early in 1949, Grandpa Hamilton died. My brother, John, was born a few months later in 1949 and not long after my brother's birth, our family moved to Ashland, Ohio to be closer to Grandma Hamilton. Mom and Dad still live in Ashland, Ohio and have four grandchildren and two great granddaughters.

My father reeceived a European ribbon with four battle stars, a Good Conduct medal, a Combat Infantryman's medal, and the Bronze Star.

I would like to thank my daughter-in-law, Wendy, for sharing her time and talent and David Wiesenberg and The Wooster Book Company for their kindness and expertise. It is interesting to note that the street address of The Wooster Book Company is the same address as that of my grandparents to whom my father wrote—205 West Liberty Street.

I would also like to extend a big thank you to Lorraine Castor for the wonderful help and encouragement she gave me at the very beginning of this project.

And most of all—Thank you Dad for writing those letters, and for coming home. We love you!

Epilogue

Remembering …

Battle of the Bulge
Sometime in January 1945

Six of us went on patrol into Echternach, Luxembourg, about 2 A.M. to try and find out how many Germans were still holed up there. Very little resistance. Captured 4 Germans. Went through 10 or 12 buildings looking for loot. Lots of broken dishes and pots and pans all banged up or broken. I had 2 or 3 nice linen table clothes and some silverware, which I brought back to our headquarters and put in my duffel bag. That was the last time I saw my duffel bag. Whoever saw me put that stuff in my bag wanted it more than I did.

When we came back to headquarters on this patrol we saw 2 signs that read ACHTUNG MINEN (Attention Mines). Either the Germans had moved the minefield or we were very lucky. While we were in Echternach we came across some hot cereal and other food. It looked good but we were trained to not touch it. Could be booby-trapped.

The next night our company moved down into some of the buildings into the cellars which were better than out in the cold. The weather was cold but no snow. When we got back to headquarters on this patrol I found out my field jacket had been torn right across the front of my belt. Sarge told me I was lucky. A bullet had gone through my jacket. It was probably shot by one of the Germans we captured. When we were in the cellars at

Echternach we couldn't have any heat because the smoke would give away our position.

The next night we left Echternach, crossed the Saar river in boats (where they came from I don't know). Ten or 12 men in a boat. Water very swift, river about 15 or 20 yards wide. Out of boats onto flat land advancing about 15 yards and then started up a hill, at least 2 or 3 two-story houses high. About halfway up I sat down to rest, we were crawling on hands and knees when I sat down I took off my helmet and it started to roll back down the hill. I had to get up and run down the hill after my helmet. It finally hit a tree and stopped rolling. I got my helmet with the inner liner still in it and had to climb back up the hill and catch up with the rest of our company. When we got to the top of the hill we saw a big farm house and barn with German soldiers walking around, not knowing we were there. They were not carrying rifles so we were ordered to rush them and capture them without gunfire if possible. When they saw us they were surprised and told our Lieutenant that we had come too far, that the war was back down at the bottom of the hill where we just came from. We must have had 15 or 20 prisoners. We locked them in the barn, we went into the house posting guards outside to get some rest. A while later we were woke up by a loud commotion outside and the Germans we had put in the barn broke out and captured our guards and surrounded the house we were in. Not one shot had been fired. Our lieutenant talked to the German officer in charge and convinced him to not show any resistance. I think the Germans were glad that we had come along and now the war was over as far as they were concerned. Later that day more American G.I.s came along and relieved us and took the prisoners back to our command post. I have no idea where that was or how far away it was, but it could have been a mile away or less.

It started to snow and we could hardly see ahead of us so we were told to dig in and wait. I dug a slit trench just deep enough to get me below the surface of the ground. I was too tired to go any deeper and too scared to quit digging. I had guard duty, I think, from midnight to 2 A.M. While on guard duty we were shelled very hard and a number of times I had to hit the ground when I heard shells coming in close and it felt like some of the shell fragments flew over me pretty close.

While we were in this position outside of Luxembourg we were surrounded for 5 days and 6 nights. There was no way you could move in the daytime and at night it wasn't much better. We couldn't eat anything in the daylight and our sergeants passed out C-rations and K-rations to us at night. While in this position, not being able to move much, you couldn't even set up to eat and relieving yourself got to be quite an adventure. We were finally relieved by the 5th infantry division who broke through the German lines and got to us.

February 12, 1945

My feet and socks and shoes were cold and partially frozen. I would take my shoes off at night and put them in my lap and curl up and try to get some sleep and warm up my shoes at the same time. Later on I heard that the G.I.s were issued some kind of lace up boot that came up halfway to their knees.

My feet and ankles turned black and blue, mostly black, and swelled so much I couldn't lace my shoes. I was taken back to an aid station by a medic who helped me walk. The aid station transferred me to the 106th Battalion Hospital in Thionville, France, on the 12th of February 1945. I was in a big ward of about 20 or 30 men with beds on both sides and 5 or 6 beds down the middle. That first night I woke up and had to go to the bathroom but I couldn't walk there. There was a big G.I. in the bed next to me and he heard me trying to get up and he said he would help me. He had his left arm in a sling but he stooped down in front of me and told me to wrap my arms around his neck and he would take me piggyback to the latrine. He had a shrapnel wound in his left arm. After getting me back in bed he bragged to the nurse how he could do her job with only one arm. On February 19, 1945, I was taken to the 8th Air Force Evacuation Hospital in Paris, France. On the 20th of February 1945, we were being moved again. We were in a big room at the Evacuation Hospital and we had tags around our necks and laying on stretchers. Some G.I.s were staying in France and some were going to the United Kingdom (England). When they got to me my card was blank and no one knew where I should go so I pointed into the room where the G.I.s going to England were and one of the hospital attendants wrote U.K. on my card and I was on my way to England.

The Bronze Star is awarded to any person who, while serving in any capacity in or with the Army of the United States, on or after December 7, 1941, distinguished himself by heroic or meritorious achievement in connection with military operations against an enemy of the United States.